CREATIVE WRITING FOR
HIGH SCHOOL : GRADE 9-12

MASTER PERSUASIVE, CREATIVE, AND ANALYTICAL WRITING SKILLS WITH HIGH SCHOOL CREATIVE WRITING PROMPTS WORKBOOK FOR TEENS

DR. FANATOMY

copyright@ dr. fanatomy 2025

All rights reserved. No part of this publication may be reproduced, distributed, or transmitted in any form or by any means, including photocopying, recording, or other electronic or mechanical methods, without the prior written permission of the publisher, except in the case of brief quotations embodied in critical reviews and certain other noncommercial uses permitted by copyright law.

This book is a work of non-fiction, and any resemblance to actual persons, living or dead, or actual events is purely coincidental.

The information and techniques described in this book are intended for educational and informational purposes only. The author and publisher shall not be held liable for any injury, damage, or loss arising from using or misusing the information presented in this book.

While every effort has been made to ensure the accuracy of the information contained within this book, the author and publisher make no warranties or representations express or implied, about the completeness, accuracy, reliability, suitability, or availability with respect to the contents of this book for any purpose. The use of any information provided in this book is at the reader's own risk.

Bonus Booklet For You!

With great pleasure, I warmly welcome you to purchase the book. Congratulations on stepping towards improving yourself and developing the skills necessary to thrive as a teenager and beyond.

Below is a surprise gift for you!

Download it from the link (or scan the QR code below)
https://bit.ly/TeeNavigationBonus

TABLE OF CONTENTS

1. INTRODUCTION TO CREATIVE WRITING (Pg:4-10)

What is Creative Writing?
- Definition and significance in self-expression.
- Differences between creative, persuasive, analytical, and professional writing.
- Examples of creative writing formats: short stories, poems, and scripts.

Why Creative Writing Matters
- Enhancing imagination, critical thinking, and communication skills.
- Its role in academic achievement and career readiness.
- Real-world applications, from storytelling to problem-solving.

How to Use This Book
- Overview of chapters and high school writing prompts.
- Tips for setting goals and tracking progress.
- Encouragement to explore and experiment with different styles.

Trivia Corner
Activity Corner 1

2. UNDERSTANDING WRITING FUNDAMENTALS (Pg:11-18)

The Building Blocks of Writing
- Grammar, punctuation, and sentence structure basics.
- Why clarity and coherence are essential.

Crafting Strong Paragraphs
- How to create compelling topic sentences and supporting details.
- Practice: Rewrite a weak paragraph to improve flow and meaning.

Mastering Descriptive Language
- Using sensory details, metaphors, and similes for vivid descriptions.
- Practice: Write a description of your favorite place using all five senses.

Trivia Corner
Activity Corner 2

3. WRITING FOR PERSUASION (Pg:19-27)

What is Persuasive Writing?
- Defining the goal: Convincing the audience.
- Examples: Opinion articles, speeches, and advertisements.

Building a Strong Persuasive Argument
- Developing a clear thesis with logical evidence and emotional appeal.
- Practice: Write a persuasive essay on a school-related issue.

High School Writing Prompts
- "Convince your school to adopt a four-day week."
- "Write a speech advocating for environmental awareness."

- *Trivia Corner*
- *Activity Corner 3*

4. EXPLORING ANALYTICAL WRITING (Pg: 28-36)

What is Analytical Writing?
- Breaking down ideas and understanding themes.
- Common examples: Book reviews, literary analyses, and essays.

Analyzing Texts Effectively
- Identifying the main idea, tone, and purpose.
- Recognizing supporting evidence and structure.

Crafting Strong Analytical Arguments
- Building clear and well-supported paragraphs.
- Practice: Analyze a provided short story for its underlying themes.

- Trivia Corner
- Activity Corner 4

5. CREATIVE STORYTELLING (Pg: 37-45)

The Key Elements of Storytelling
- Exploring plot, characters, conflict, setting, and theme.
- Case studies: What makes certain stories timeless?

Developing Characters with Depth
- Creating dynamic character profiles and realistic dialogue.
- Practice: Write a dialogue between two characters with clashing views.

Structuring Your Story
- Plot arcs: Beginning, rising action, climax, and resolution.
- Practice: Develop a story outline based on a creative writing prompt.

Trivia Corner
Activity Corner 5

6. CREATIVE WRITING FOR THE FUTURE (Pg: 46-58)

Creative Writing for the Future: Embrace Innovation and Captivate Audiences
- Introduction: Writing for Tomorrow's World

Digital Storytelling: Captivate Your Audience Across Platforms

Your Turn! Get Creative!

Deep Dive: The Building Blocks of Digital Storytelling
- Interactive Fiction: Where Readers Take Control
- Blogging and Microblogging: Share Your Voice with the World
- Scriptwriting for Video Content: Bring Your Stories to Life on Screen
- Flash Fiction and Microfiction: Tell Powerful Stories in a Nutshell
- Visual Poetry: Where Words Take Shape
- Collaborative Writing: The Power of Teamwork
- Podcast Storytelling: Bring Your Stories to Life Through Sound
- Collaborative Writing: The Power of Teamwork
- Podcast Storytelling: Bring Your Stories to Life Through Sound
- Environmental Storytelling: Connecting with Nature Through Narrative
- AI-Enhanced Writing: Unleash Your Creativity

- Trivia Corner
- Activity Corner 6

7. WRITING FOR THE DIGITAL AGE: COPYWRITING ESSENTIALS

What is Copywriting? (Pg: 59-66)
- Definition and significance in marketing and communication.
- Examples: Social media posts, ads, emails, and web content.

Key Principles of Effective Copywriting
- Writing headlines that grab attention.
- Crafting concise, engaging, and persuasive messages.
- The importance of understanding the audience and brand voice.

Copywriting Techniques and Practice
- Using power words and calls to action (CTAs).
- Practice: Write a compelling social media ad for a fictional product.
- Exercise: Create an email pitch for a school fundraiser.

How Copywriting Prepares You for the Future
- Skills for entrepreneurship, digital marketing, and content creation.

Trivia Corner
Activity Corner 7

8. HIGH SCHOOL WRITING PROMPTS FOR CREATIVITY AND GROWTH (Pg: 67-74)

What are Writing Prompts?
- How prompts spark creativity and hone writing skills.
- Tips for using prompts effectively in daily practice.

Themed Writing Prompts
- Adventure: "Write about discovering a secret passage in your school."
- Personal growth: "Describe a time you learned a difficult lesson."
- Mystery: "Your town loses power, and strange things start happening."

Freewriting Challenges
- Timed prompts for spontaneous creativity.
- Practice: Write for 15 minutes about a random object in your room.

Trivia Corner
Activity Corner 8

9. LEVEL UP YOUR ONLINE PRESENCE WITH CREATIVE WRITING

Why Brand Yourself Online (Pg: 75-85)

- Understanding Your Online Brand
- Tips for using prompts effectively in daily practice.

The Art of Selling Yourself with Creative Writing

Tips for Writing Sales Copy That Sells

- Social Media Strategies for Creative Writers
- Scaling Your Brand
- Exercises: Level Up Your Online Presence
- Trivia Corner
- Activity Corner 9

10. CREATIVE WRITING FOR THE DIGITAL AGE: MODERN APPLICATIONS AND EXERCISES (Pg: 86-100)

Tweet
LinkedIn Post
Sales Page Copywriting
Digital Storytelling
Blogging
YouTube Video Script Writing
Gamified Content Creation
Educational Content Development
Technical Writing
Branded Storytelling
Trivia Corner
Activity Corner 10

ACTIVITY ANSWERS (Pg: 101-110)

CONCLUSION: CREATIVE WRITING FOR HIGH SCHOOL STUDENTS (Pg: 111 - 112)

APPENDIX (Pg: 113 -115)

- *Appendix -A: Creative Writing Formats and Their Characteristics*
- *Appendix -B: Grammar and Punctuation Tips for Creative Writing*
- *Appendix -C: Writing Tips for Effective Storytelling*
- *Appendix - D: Helpful Writing Resources*
- *Appendix - E : Career Opportunities in Writing and Content Creation*

1. Introduction to Creative Writing

What is Creative Writing?

Definition and Significance in Self-Expression

Creative writing is a form of writing that transcends mere facts and information. It emphasizes imagination, originality, and self-expression. Unlike technical or academic writing, creative writing allows individuals to explore emotions, tell stories, and create fictional worlds.

Example: Writing a short story about a young detective solving a mystery in a futuristic city.

Differences Between Creative, Persuasive, Analytical, and Professional Writing :

Reading comprehension involves understanding, interpreting, and analyzing written texts; it's about reading words and grasping their meaning, purpose, and connections.

Writing Type	Purpose	Example
Creative Writing	To entertain, inspire, or evoke emotions	A poem about overcoming challenges
Persuasive Writing	To convince the audience of a specific viewpoint	An essay arguing for renewable energy usage
Analytical Writing	To examine and interpret information	A book review analyzing themes and symbols
Professional Writing	To convey information clearly and efficiently	A resume or business email

Examples of Creative Writing Formats :

Short Stories: Compact tales that often center around a single theme or character arc.

- **Example**: A story about a magical forest that grants wishes but at a price.

Poems: Expressive works that use rhythm, imagery, and metaphor.
- Example: A poem describing the beauty of a sunrise in winter.

Scripts: Written for performance, including plays, screenplays, and dialogues.
- Example: A script for a play about a group of students starting a band.

Why Creative Writing Matters

Enhancing Imagination, Critical Thinking, and Communication Skills
Creative writing fosters the ability to think beyond the ordinary. Writers imagine new worlds, develop characters, and solve problems through storytelling.

Example Activity: Write a story where the main character must solve a problem using an unconventional tool, like a book or a shadow.

Its Role in Academic Achievement and Career Readiness

Creative writing builds transferable skills, such as:

- Critical Thinking: Analyzing characters and plot developments.
- Communication: Expressing complex ideas clearly and engagingly.
- Problem-Solving: Crafting narratives with logical resolutions.

Fact: According to a study by the National Writing Project, students who engage in creative writing perform better in academic subjects like reading comprehension and critical analysis.

Real-World Applications

Creative writing isn't just for authors; it's valuable in many fields:

- Marketing: Writing engaging content for advertisements.
- Journalism: Crafting compelling human-interest stories.
- Education: Creating lesson plans or educational resources.

Example Table: Career Paths and Creative Writing Skills

Career	How Creative Writing Helps
Marketing	Crafting compelling taglines and brand stories
Journalism	Writing engaging feature articles
Education	Designing innovative teaching materials and stories
Game Design	Creating immersive worlds and narratives for video games

The Future Relevance of Creative Writing in Career Development for High School Students

Career Path	Role of Creative Writing	Example in Action	Future Relevance
Content Creation	Developing engaging content for blogs, social media, and multimedia platforms.	Writing an inspiring blog post about climate change or creating a viral campaign script for a new product.	Growing demand for personalized, creative digital content in a globalized and tech-driven world.
Marketing and Branding	Crafting compelling brand stories, advertisements, and promotional materials.	Writing a catchy slogan for an eco-friendly brand or a script for a product launch.	With increasing competition, storytelling is critical for brand differentiation and audience connection.
Game Development	Building immersive narratives and character backstories for video games.	Designing the plot for an open-world fantasy game where players influence outcomes based on decisions.	The booming gaming industry requires innovative storytelling to enhance user experiences.
Film and Television	Writing screenplays, scripts, or storyboards for shows, movies, or web series.	Penning the script for a short film about artificial intelligence ethics.	Streaming platforms and independent cinema are creating more opportunities for original storytelling.

Publishing	Authoring books, poetry collections, or short stories for traditional or self-publishing markets.	Writing a young adult novel about overcoming adversity in a dystopian society.	Increased access to publishing platforms enables wider outreach for new writers.
Education	Creating innovative lesson plans, educational stories, and academic resources.	Writing a creative short story to teach middle school students about historical events.	Education requires dynamic approaches to engage tech-savvy students in the 21st century.
Technology	Designing interactive user manuals, tutorials, and AI-generated narratives.	Creating a user guide for a virtual reality headset or training prompts for AI models like chatbots.	The intersection of tech and creativity is pivotal for innovation in UX/UI design and AI development.
Entrepreneurship	Crafting business proposals, vision statements, and inspiring pitches.	Writing an engaging pitch for a startup seeking to revolutionize renewable energy solutions.	Entrepreneurship thrives on vision and communication—creative writing boosts both.
Therapy and Wellness	Using storytelling and journaling as therapeutic tools in counseling or mental health initiatives.	Developing a guided journal for teens to manage stress or writing relatable stories to aid emotional healing.	Mental health awareness will drive the need for creative therapeutic tools.
Artificial Intelligence	Developing creative prompts for training AI, writing conversational scripts for chatbots, and curating content.	Providing dialogue scenarios for AI virtual assistants to improve conversational nuances.	AI systems rely on well-crafted human inputs for natural language processing and development.

TRIVIA CORNER

- **Longest Novel:** Marcel Proust's In Search of Lost Time exceeds 1.2 million words, holding the record for the longest novel.
- **First Mystery Story:** Edgar Allan Poe's The Murders in the Rue Morgue (1841) introduced the modern detective genre.
- **World Poetry Day:** Celebrated on March 21, it highlights poetry's role in fostering creativity and culture.
- **Rowling's Rejections:** Harry Potter was rejected 12 times before becoming a global success, proving perseverance pays off.
- **Creative Writing in Gaming:** The Last of Us showcases how strong storytelling enhances gaming experiences.
- **Origin of "Poetry":** Derived from the Greek poiesis ("to create"), reflecting poetry's essence of creativity.

ACTIVITY CORNER 1
Introduction to Creative Writing

1. Identify the Writing Type

*Instructions: Read the prompts below and identify the type of writing being described. Choose from: **Creative Writing, Analytical Writing, Persuasive Writing, Informative Writing**.*

Prompts:

1. A story about a teenager who discovers a magical library.
2. An article explaining how photosynthesis works.
3. An essay arguing why schools should adopt renewable energy.
4. A book review analyzing the themes of friendship and betrayal.

2. Choose the Correct Format

Instructions: Match the following scenarios to the most appropriate creative writing format.

Prompts:

1. A script for a school play about teamwork.
2. A short piece about the first day of high school.
3. A poem describing the changing seasons.
4. A blog post sharing tips on organizing a study schedule.

3. Complete the Sentence

Instructions: Fill in the blanks with the correct terms related to creative writing.

Prompts:

1. A _____ is a compact fictional narrative often focusing on a single theme.
2. The _____ of a poem refers to its rhythmic pattern and flow.
3. A _____ is designed for performance, incorporating dialogue and stage directions.
4. _____ writing is often used to explore personal thoughts and experiences.

ACTIVITY CORNER 1

Introduction to Creative Writing

4. True or False

*Instructions: Determine whether the following statements are **true or false**.*

Prompts:

1. Creative writing focuses solely on factual information.
2. A poem can use imagery and metaphor to express ideas.
3. Analytical writing is primarily used for entertainment.
4. A screenplay includes elements such as dialogue and stage directions.

5. Identify the Purpose

Instructions: Read the following writing excerpts and identify their purpose: **to entertain, to inform, to persuade, to analyze.**

Prompts:

1. "Renewable energy is the key to a sustainable future. Here's why we should act now."
2. "The sunset painted the sky with hues of orange and pink, a canvas of nature's beauty."
3. "This novel explores the theme of resilience through the protagonist's journey."
4. "Volcanoes form when magma rises to the Earth's surface. Here's how it happens."

6. Match Terms with Their Definitions

Instructions: Match the terms in Column A with their definitions in Column B.

Column A	Column B
1. Creative Writing	a) Writing that conveys information or facts
2. Analytical Writing	b) Writing that breaks down and examines a subject
3. Persuasive Writing	c) Writing intended to convince the audience
4. Informative Writing	d) Writing that focuses on imagination and storytelling

2. Building a Strong Foundation: Writing Fundamentals

Writing is much more than stringing words together; it's a way to express yourself, share your ideas, and reach your goals. Like constructing a building, effective writing starts with a solid foundation. This chapter introduces the essential building blocks: grammar, punctuation, sentence structure, clarity, and descriptive language. With these tools, you'll unlock your potential as a skilled and confident writer.

Grammar: The Rules of the Road

Grammar is the backbone of clear communication. Just as traffic laws ensure drivers navigate safely, grammar rules help your ideas flow smoothly, ensuring clarity and precision in your writing.

Parts of Speech: The Essentials

Part of Speech	Definition	Examples
Noun	Names a person, place, thing, or idea	student, city, book, happiness
Verb	Shows action or state of being	run, eat, think, is, are
Adjective	Describes a noun	beautiful, tall, happy
Adverb	Describes a verb, adjective, or adverb	quickly, loudly, very

Subject-Verb Agreement

To keep your sentences grammatically correct, the subject and verb must agree in number.

- **Singular subject**: The dog barks.
- **Plural subject**: The dogs bark.

Punctuation: The Road Signs of Writing

Punctuation marks guide readers through your writing, ensuring clarity and readability. Misplacing a comma or period can change the meaning of a sentence entirely.

Key Punctuation Marks

- **Commas**
    - Separate items in a list: I like apples, oranges, and bananas.
    - Set off introductory phrases: After the rain, we went for a walk.
    - Join independent clauses with conjunctions: I finished my homework, and then I watched a movie.

- **Periods and Question Marks**
    - Use a period to end a declarative sentence: The sun is shining.
    - Use a question mark to end an interrogative sentence: Are you going to the party?

Sentence Structure: Building Strong Foundations

Strong sentences are the building blocks of powerful paragraphs. Using a variety of sentence structures makes your writing more dynamic and engaging.

Sentence Type	Definition	Example
Simple Sentence	Contains one independent clause	The cat sat on the mat.
Compound Sentence	Combines two independent clauses with a conjunction	The cat sat on the mat, and the dog barked.
Complex Sentence	Includes one independent clause and one dependent clause	After the rain stopped, the children played.

Clarity and Coherence: Making Your Writing Understandable

Clear and coherent writing ensures your ideas are easy to follow. Confusing or disorganized writing can distract readers from your message.

Tips for Clarity

Use precise language: Replace vague words with specific ones.
- Vague: "The thing was amazing."
- Precise: "The rollercoaster was thrilling."

Avoid jargon and slang: Tailor your language to your audience.

Organize logically: Present your thoughts in a clear sequence.

Crafting Powerful Paragraphs

A paragraph should feel like a mini-essay, with a clear structure:
1. Topic Sentence: Introduces the main idea.
2. Supporting Sentences: Provide evidence, examples, or explanations.
3. Concluding Sentence: Summarizes or reinforces the key idea.

Example Paragraph

Topic Sentence: Social media has revolutionized the way we communicate.

Supporting Sentences:

- Platforms like Instagram and Twitter let us connect instantly across the globe.
- Businesses use social media to reach new audiences and grow their brands.
- Activists amplify their causes using viral hashtags.
- Concluding Sentence: Social media is a transformative tool for global communication in the 21st century.

Descriptive Language: Bringing Your Writing to Life

Descriptive language transforms writing from ordinary to extraordinary. It helps readers visualize, feel, and connect with your story.

Using Sensory Details

Engage the five senses (sight, sound, smell, taste, and touch) to create vivid imagery.

- Example: The aroma of freshly baked cookies wafted through the warm kitchen, mingling with the cheerful crackle of the fireplace.

Incorporating Figurative Language

- **Metaphors:** Compare two things directly. Life is a rollercoaster.
- **Similes:** Compare using "like" or "as." Her laughter was like a melody

Practice

Topic Sentence: Social media has revolutionized the way we communicate. Write a paragraph describing your favorite meal using sensory details.

Create a metaphor or simile for:
- A thunderstorm
- The feeling of excitement

Mastering the fundamentals of writing is like building a sturdy house: with a strong foundation, the possibilities are endless. By focusing on grammar, punctuation, sentence structure, clarity, and descriptive language, you'll gain the confidence to tackle any writing challenge.

These skills are not just for high school—they'll benefit you in college, the workplace, and beyond. Ready to take your writing to the next level? Let's dive into the creative world ahead!

Trivia Corner

Did you know?
- The shortest grammatically correct sentence in English is "Go." It's a simple imperative sentence with a subject implied rather than stated.

Grammar fun fact:
- The word "set" has the most definitions of any word in the English language, with over 430 different meanings listed in the Oxford English Dictionary.

Punctuation curiosity:
- The exclamation mark (!) was originally called a "note of admiration" when it first appeared in the 14th century.

Sentence structure trivia:
- The longest sentence ever published is in Victor Hugo's novel Les Misérables. It contains 823 words! (Don't try this at home in essays!)

Descriptive writing insight:
- The word "smell" is the only sense that can be used as both a noun and a verb without any change in spelling. Example: I love the smell of roses (noun) and I can smell the roses (verb).

Topic sentence fact:
- A great topic sentence is like a headline in a newspaper. It grabs attention and gives you a preview of what's coming next.

Language evolution:
- Many punctuation marks we use today originated from medieval scribes. For example, the comma evolved from a Greek mark called a "komma," meaning "a piece cut off."

Metaphor magic:
- Shakespeare is credited with inventing many metaphors still in use today, like "break the ice" (The Taming of the Shrew) and "all the world's a stage" (As You Like It).

Writing mechanics:
- The semicolon (;) is often misunderstood. It's used to connect closely related ideas within a sentence and was invented by Italian printer Aldus Manutius in 1494.

Power of words:
- The word "okay" (or OK) is one of the most recognized terms worldwide. It started as a humorous abbreviation for "oll korrect" (a playful misspelling of "all correct") in the 1830s.

ACTIVITY CORNER 2

1) Grammar and Parts of Speech (MCQ)

Identify the part of speech of the bolded word in the sentence:

1) The **bright** sun shone through the window.
- a) Noun
- b) Verb
- c) Adjective
- d) Adverb

2) She **quickly** ran to catch the bus.
- a) Noun
- b) Verb
- c) Adjective
- d) Adverb

3) The **team** worked hard to win the championship.
- a) Adjective
- b) Pronoun
- c) Noun
- d) Adverb

4) They **played** soccer in the park yesterday.
- a) Verb
- b) Noun
- c) Adjective
- d) Adverb

5) He bought a **beautiful** painting for his living room.
- a) Verb
- b) Adjective
- c) Adverb
- d) Noun

2) Match the Sentence Structure (Match the Following)

Match each sentence type with its correct example:

ACTIVITY CORNER 2

Sentence Type	Example
1. Simple Sentence	a. After the storm passed, we went outside to play.
2. Compound Sentence	b. I went to the store, and I bought some milk.
3. Complex Sentence	c. The dog barked loudly.
4. Compound-Complex Sentence	d. When I arrived, the show had started, but I still enjoyed it.

3) Punctuation Practice (Fill in the Blanks)

Add the missing punctuation to these sentences:

1. We visited Paris London and Rome during our vacation.
2. After the movie we went to grab some dinner.
3. She loves reading but she also enjoys painting.
4. Are you coming to the party tomorrow
5. I can't believe it's already December

4) Build a Paragraph

Below is a disorganized paragraph. Place the sentences in the correct order:

Sentence	Position (1-5)
Social media platforms like Instagram and TikTok allow users to share videos instantly.	
Social media is a transformative tool in today's world.	
These platforms have also become essential for businesses to reach new audiences.	
People can connect with family and friends regardless of distance.	
It has revolutionized the way we communicate and share ideas.	

3. Writing for Persuasion

Writing for Persuasion

Persuasive writing is one of the most valuable skills you can develop in high school. It empowers you to express opinions, inspire action, and spark meaningful change in the world around you. Whether crafting an essay, delivering a speech, or designing an advertisement, mastering persuasive writing is essential for academic success, career growth, and everyday life.

What is Persuasive Writing?

Persuasive writing is the art of convincing an audience to adopt a belief, take action, or consider a new perspective. It combines logic, emotional appeal, and credibility to create a compelling argument.

Goals of Persuasive Writing

Goal	Description	Example
Convince	Persuade your audience to adopt a belief.	Writing an essay supporting renewable energy.
Inspire Action	Motivate the audience to take specific steps.	A speech encouraging students to recycle.
Raise Awareness	Highlight an issue or topic.	A social media post about climate change.

Examples of Persuasive Writing

Opinion Articles: These appear in newspapers or blogs, offering a strong viewpoint.
- Example: Why High School Should Start Later in the Morning.

Speeches: Aimed at inspiring or challenging audiences.
- Example: Martin Luther King Jr.'s "I Have a Dream" speech.

Advertisements: Designed to sell ideas or products.
- Example: A commercial demonstrating how a product can save time.

Building a Strong Persuasive Argument

A persuasive argument is built on three pillars: a clear thesis, solid evidence, and emotional appeal.

(a) Developing a Clear Thesis

Your thesis is the central idea of your argument. It should be:

- **Specific**: Avoid vague statements.
- **Instead of**: "Social media is bad."
- **Try:** "Excessive social media use harms teenagers' mental health."
- **Debatable**: Choose topics that inspire discussion.
- **Actionable**: Suggest a clear solution or call to action.

Example Thesis: Schools should adopt a four-day week to improve student well-being and academic performance.

(b) Using Logical Evidence

Support your thesis with reliable evidence:

- **Facts and Data:** Use statistics and research findings.
- **Example:** "Studies show a four-day school week reduces student stress by 30%."
- **Real-World Examples:** Share relevant instances.
- **Example:** "In Colorado, schools that implemented a four-day week reported improved attendance and cost savings."
- **Expert Opinions:** Cite credible sources.

Example: "According to Dr. Jane Doe, shorter weeks enhance academic focus."

3. Appealing to Emotions

Connect with your audience on a personal level:

- **Anecdotes:** Share relatable stories.

Example: "As a student, I often feel exhausted by Friday. A shorter week would give us the rest we need to excel.

- **Vivid Language**: Create a mental image.
Example: "Imagine a world where students are energized and engaged every day."

High School Writing Prompts

Prompt 1: Convince Your School to Adopt a Four-Day Week

Practice Question: Write a persuasive essay advocating for a four-day school week. Include a clear thesis, logical evidence, and emotional appeal.

Example Response:

Thesis: Schools should implement a four-day week to enhance student well-being and save resources.

Logical Evidence:
- A four-day week reduces stress by providing an extra day for rest.
- Schools save money on transportation and utilities.
- Districts with a four-day week saw test scores improve by 15%.

Emotional Appeal:
- "Many students feel overwhelmed. An extra day off could restore balance and help us perform better."

Conclusion:
- "By adopting a four-day week, schools can foster a healthier, happier, and more successful environment."

Prompt 2: Advocate for Environmental Awareness

Practice Question: Draft a speech encouraging your school to start a recycling program.

Example Response:
- **Opening Line**: "Every plastic bottle you recycle is one less clogging our oceans."
- **Thesis**: Recycling programs are essential for protecting the environment and reducing waste.

Key Points:

- **Facts:** "The average American produces 4.4 pounds of waste daily."
- **Examples:** "Schools in California cut waste by 50% with recycling programs."
- **Emotional Appeal:** "Think about our future. Do we want our planet to look like a landfill?"
- **Closing Line:** "Together, we can make a difference. Let's start recycling today."

Practical Tools for Persuasive Writing

Logical vs. Emotional Appeals

Type of Appeal	Definition	Example
Logical Appeal	Uses facts, data, and reasoning.	Recycling reduces landfill waste by 30% annually.
Emotional Appeal	Evokes feelings to connect with the audience.	Imagine a world where beaches are clean and forests thrive.

Persuasive Writing Checklist

Before submitting your work, ask:
- Is my thesis clear, specific, and debatable?
- Have I included solid evidence (facts, examples, and expert opinions)?
- Have I appealed to the emotions of my audience effectively?
- Does my conclusion reinforce my argument?
- Is my writing organized, error-free, and engaging?

Conclusion: The Power of Persuasion

Persuasive writing is a vital skill that will serve you in school, your career, and beyond. By practicing the techniques in this chapter, you can craft arguments that inspire change and make an impact.

Remember:
- Words have power—use them wisely.
- Practice regularly to refine your skills.
- Approach opposing viewpoints respectfully to build credibility.

So, what will you persuade others to believe or do today?

Trivia Corner

- **Aristotle's Persuasion Formula:** Aristotle, the renowned philosopher, identified three key elements of persuasion: ethos (credibility), pathos (emotion), and logos (logic).

- **Shortest Persuasive Speech:** Abraham Lincoln's Gettysburg Address, a cornerstone of American history, is a powerful example of persuasion in just 272 words.

- **First Printed Advertisement:** The first known printed advertisement appeared in England in 1477, promoting a book of prayers.

- **The Rule of Three:** This classic rhetorical device, exemplified by phrases like "life, liberty, and the pursuit of happiness," often enhances the persuasive power of ideas.

- **The Power of Repetition:** The "mere exposure effect" suggests that repeated exposure to a message can increase its persuasiveness.

- **"Just Do It":** Nike's iconic slogan, while its exact origin is debated, exemplifies the power of concise and impactful persuasive language.

- **The Impact of Emotions:** Research suggests that emotional appeals can be highly effective in persuasion, particularly in advertising, as they tap into our desires and values.

- **A Long History of Persuasion Contests:** Essay contests have a long history in education, fostering critical thinking and persuasive writing skills in students.

- **The Influence of Social Media:** Social media platforms have significantly amplified the reach and impact of persuasive messages, influencing purchasing decisions and shaping public opinion.

- **The Psychology of Color:** While the specific impact varies, colors like red (urgency) and blue (trust) can subtly influence our perceptions and responses to persuasive messages.

🎯 ACTIVITY CORNER 3

Activity 1: Multiple Choice Questions

Question 1: What is the primary goal of a thesis statement in persuasive writing?
- A. To entertain the reader
- B. To present the writer's main argument
- C. To include emotional anecdotes
- D. To summarize the conclusion

Question 2: Which of the following is an example of an emotional appeal?
- A. "A four-day school week reduces costs by 30% annually."
- B. "Imagine waking up refreshed and excited for school every day."
- C. "Research shows students perform better with more rest."
- D. "Dr. Smith recommends this policy based on a study."

Question 3: Which element is NOT a part of persuasive writing?
- A. Clear thesis
- B. Facts and data
- C. A neutral tone throughout
- D. Emotional appeals

Question 4: Which example best demonstrates logical evidence?
- A. "It's heartbreaking to see so many students overwhelmed."
- B. "In a survey, 78% of students supported healthier lunch options."
- C. "Imagine a world where every student feels well-rested."
- D. "Schools should make students happy, no matter the cost."

- Question 5: Which is a purpose of persuasive writing?
- A. To entertain an audience with a story
- B. To bring attention to an issue or motivate action
- C. To teach historical events
- D. To describe a natural phenomenon

ACTIVITY CORNER 3

Activity 2 : Match the Following

Instructions: Match each term with its correct description:

Terms	Descriptions
A. Thesis Statement	1. Using emotions to connect with the audience
B. Logical Evidence	2. The central argument of your persuasive piece
C. Emotional Appeal	3. Facts, data, or statistics supporting the argument
D. Raise Awareness	4. A goal to bring attention to a critical issue

Activity 3 : Prompt Challenges

Prompt 1: Convince Your School to Extend Recess

Write a paragraph persuading your school principal to increase recess time. Your paragraph must include:
- A clear thesis statement
- Logical evidence
- An emotional appeal

Prompt 2: Persuade Your Family to Get a Pet

Write a speech to persuade your family to adopt a dog. Include:
- A clear benefit of having a dog
- At least one statistic
- A personal anecdote

🎯 ACTIVITY CORNER 3

Activity 4 : Fill in the blanks

1. The main argument of a persuasive essay is called the _____ statement.
2. _____ evidence includes facts, statistics, and data that support your argument.
3. Emotional appeals often use vivid language to create a sense of _____ in the reader.
4. Persuasive writing is most effective when it combines logical evidence and _____ appeals.
5. The purpose of a _____ paragraph is to summarize the main points and restate the thesis.

Activity 5 : Prompt Challenge: Match the Following

Instructions: Match the persuasive writing concepts in Column A with their correct descriptions in Column B.

Column A
1. Thesis Statement
2. Logical Appeal
3. Emotional Appeal
4. Anecdote
5. Call to Action

Column B
a. A brief personal story used to connect with the audience.
b. The main argument or central idea of your essay.
c. Encourages the audience to take specific steps or actions.
d. Uses facts, data, and evidence to support an argument.
e. Evokes feelings to create a connection with the audience.

4. Exploring Analytical Writing

What is Analytical Writing?

Imagine you're watching a movie. You don't just watch it; you think about the director's choices—the music, the lighting, how the characters interact. You might even try to understand the deeper message the movie conveys. That's analytical thinking in action!

Analytical writing is similar. It's not just about summarizing information but breaking it down and exploring deeper meanings.

Key Aspects of Analytical Writing:

- **Breaking Down Complex Ideas:** Like dissecting a frog in science class, you examine the parts of a text (a book, article, speech, or even a song).

- **Understanding Connections**: You figure out how the parts contribute to the whole.

- **Discovering Deeper Meanings**: You uncover hidden messages, themes, and assumptions.

Common Examples of Analytical Writing

Type of Analysis	Real-World Example
Literary Analysis	Exploring how the green light in The Great Gatsby symbolizes hope and unattainable dreams.
Historical Analysis	Examining the causes of the American Revolution and its impact on democracy worldwide.
Scientific Analysis	Interpreting lab results to understand how fertilizers affect plant growth.
Film Analysis	Analyzing Alfred Hitchcock's use of suspense in Psycho.

Key Steps to Analytical Writing

- **Understand the Text:**
    - Read actively: Highlight, take notes, and ask questions.
    - Identify the main idea: What is the central argument?
    - Determine tone and purpose: Is it serious, humorous, critical?

- **Analyze the Evidence:**
    - Look for supporting details: Quotes, data, or examples that back the main idea.
    - Examine techniques: How does the author use language (imagery, word choice, tone)?

- **Develop Your Argument:**
    - Create a thesis statement: This is your main claim or argument.
    - Organize logically: Use an outline to structure your essay.
    - Support with evidence: Use specific examples to prove your point.

Building Strong Analytical Paragraphs

Each paragraph in your analytical essay should focus on one main idea. Use the following structure:

1. Topic Sentence: States the paragraph's main point.
2. Evidence: Includes quotes, data, or examples.
3. Analysis: Explains how the evidence supports the topic.
4. Concluding Sentence: Ties the paragraph to your overall thesis.

Example Paragraph: Literary Analysis

Prompt: How does Shakespeare use light imagery in Romeo and Juliet?

- **Topic Sentence:** Shakespeare uses light imagery in Romeo and Juliet to symbolize love and hope.

- **Evidence**: "But soft! What light through yonder window breaks? It is the east, and Juliet is the sun!" (Act II, Scene ii).

- **Analysis:** Here, Romeo compares Juliet to the sun, portraying her as a source of light, warmth, and life. This imagery emphasizes Juliet's importance in Romeo's world.

- **Concluding Sentence:** By using light as a symbol, Shakespeare highlights the transformative power of love.

Interactive Activities

1. Analyze a Song

Song: "drivers license" by Olivia Rodrigo

Themes: Heartbreak and moving on: The song explores the pain of a lost love and the difficulties of moving on from a past relationship.

Jealousy and social media: It delves into the complexities of navigating social media and witnessing your ex-partner with someone new.

Self-discovery and growth: The song portrays the emotional journey of self-discovery and healing after a significant loss.

Literary Devices: Metaphor: "And you're probably with that blonde girl / Who always made me doubt / She's so much older than me / She's everything I'm insecure about" (Comparing the "blonde girl" to her own insecurities).

Imagery: "And you're probably with that blonde girl / Who always made me doubt / She's so much older than me / She's everything I'm insecure about" (Creating vivid mental pictures of the ex-partner with someone new).

Tone: The song is predominantly melancholic and introspective, conveying feelings of sadness, regret, and longing.

Interactive Activities

2. Analyze a Song: Compare and Contrast Texts

Texts: "The Fault in Our Stars" by John Green and "Five Feet Apart" by Rachael Lippincott

Theme: Finding Love and Hope in the Face of Adversity (specifically terminal illness)
- "The Fault in Our Stars":Focuses on the intense and transformative love story between two teenagers with cancer.
- Explores themes of mortality, acceptance, and the importance of living life to the fullest.
- Emphasizes the power of humor and friendship in coping with difficult circumstances.
- "Five Feet Apart":Tells the story of two teenagers with cystic fibrosis who fall in love but are forbidden from physical contact due to the risk of infection.
- Explores themes of longing, sacrifice, and the challenges of finding joy and connection amidst limitations.
- Highlights the importance of hope and the human desire for connection.

Key Differences: Focus on Love: "The Fault in Our Stars" portrays a more passionate and all-consuming love, while "Five Feet Apart" emphasizes the longing and frustration of a love that cannot be fully realized.

Themes of Acceptance: "The Fault in Our Stars" grapples more directly with the inevitability of death and the importance of finding meaning in the face of mortality.

Tone: "The Fault in Our Stars" has a more bittersweet and melancholic tone, while "Five Feet Apart" maintains a more hopeful and uplifting tone, emphasizing the importance of finding joy in the present moment.

Interactive Activities

3. Analyze a Short Excerpt

Excerpt: "My phone buzzes constantly, a symphony of notifications. But is it really connecting me, or just isolating me in a bubble of curated perfection?"

Theme: The impact of social media on mental health and well-being.

Analysis: This excerpt highlights the potential downsides of excessive social media use. The "symphony of notifications" symbolizes the constant bombardment of information and the pressure to maintain an online persona. The question posed at the end encourages critical reflection on the true nature of connection in the digital age. It suggests that while social media can connect us with others, it can also create feelings of isolation and inadequacy due to the curated and often unrealistic portrayals of others' lives.

Additional Resources for Students

Resource	What It Offers
Purdue OWL	Guides on essay structure, thesis writing, and analysis techniques.
Khan Academy	Videos and exercises on reading comprehension and critical thinking.
SparkNotes	Analysis of themes, characters, and symbols in classic literature.

By mastering analytical writing, you'll unlock the ability to think critically, express yourself clearly, and succeed academically. Now grab your pen (or keyboard) and start exploring the deeper layers of meaning in the world around you!

Trivia Corner

- "Analysis" comes from Greek "analytikos" (to unravel). Analytical writing breaks complex ideas down for better understanding.

- "Essay" comes from French "essayer" (to try). It's an attempt to uncover deeper meanings.

- In Orwell's 1984, "doublethink" is a key analytical theme. It explores the conflict between truth and propaganda.

- Thomas Paine's Common Sense (1776) is an early example of analytical writing that fueled the American Revolution.

- Inception explores the concept of dreams within dreams, sparking analysis of reality and perception.

- Charles Darwin's "On the Origin of Species" demonstrates how analytical reasoning revolutionized science.

- In Romeo and Juliet, light and dark symbolize love and danger. Analyzing symbolism reveals hidden meanings.

- The five-paragraph essay is a teaching tool for organizing and clarifying analytical arguments.

- In Harry Potter, the Sorting Hat symbolizes personal choice vs. destiny, prompting analysis of identity and free will.

- The thesis statement is the "backbone" of an analytical essay. Without a clear thesis, analysis loses focus.

🎯 ACTIVITY CORNER 4
Activity: Exploring Analytical Writing

Activity 1: Analyzing a Social Media Post :

Scenario: Analyze the following social media post:

"Every piece of plastic recycled helps reduce ocean pollution. Let's do our part!"

(1) What is the tone of the post?

1. a) Sarcastic
2. b) Informative
3. c) Humorous
4. d) Aggressive

(2) What is the main purpose of the post?

a) Entertain readers
b) Provoke an argument
c) Inspire action
d) Share a personal story

Activity 2 Analyze a Commercial or Advertisement

Scenario: Watch a Nike ad featuring a young athlete overcoming challenges with the slogan "Just Do It."

(1) What is the primary target audience of this ad?

a) Professional athletes
b) Young athletes
c) Business executives
d) Parents

(2) What emotional appeal does the ad use to inspire viewers?

a) Humor
b) Fear
c) Motivation
d) Sadness

🎯 ACTIVITY CORNER 4

Activity: Exploring Analytical Writing

Activity 3: Dissect a Movie Scene

Scenario: Analyze The Hunger Games' Reaping Scene.

(1) What does the muted color palette of the scene symbolize?

1. a) Hope
2. b) Oppression
3. c) Celebration
4. d) Chaos

(2) What theme is explored through the dramatic tension of the scene?

a) Sacrifice for loved ones
b) The joy of competition
c) Justice in society
d) Equality among districts

Activity 4: Rewrite an Argument with Better Evidence

Scenario: Improve this weak argument: "School uniforms are good because they look nice."

Questions:

(1) Which evidence strengthens the argument most?

1. a) Uniforms create equality, reducing bullying.
2. b) Uniforms make students feel stylish.
3. c) Uniforms match school logos and colors.
4. d) Uniforms help schools look professional.

(2) Which rewritten thesis statement is best?

a) School uniforms help students look professional.
b) School uniforms promote creativity in fashion.
c) School uniforms create equality and reduce bullying.
d) School uniforms make schools stylish and trendy.

5. Creative Storytelling

Creative Storytelling for High School: Captivate Your Audience!

Ready to unleash your inner storyteller? In this chapter, we'll explore the key ingredients that make stories pop and guide you through crafting your own narratives. Buckle up, aspiring authors!

Building Blockbusters: The Essential Elements

Every great story is like a delicious pizza – it needs the right ingredients to truly shine. Here are the main components that bring your narrative to life:

Plot
The action-packed journey your characters take. Think of it as a series of connected events, with a problem (conflict) that needs to be solved.
Example: In The Maze Runner, the characters navigate a dangerous maze to uncover the truth about their world.

Characters
These are the folks (or creatures!) who drive the story forward. They should feel real, with their own personalities, strengths, weaknesses, and desires.
Example: Katniss Everdeen (The Hunger Games) is brave and resourceful, yet struggles with her emotions and sense of responsibility.

Conflict
The challenge your characters face – the obstacle they need to overcome. It could be anything from a villain to internal fears.
Example: In Inside Out, Riley's emotions grapple with the challenges of growing up.

Setting
The backdrop where your story unfolds. Is it a bustling city, a haunted mansion, or a futuristic spaceship? The setting creates the atmosphere.
Example: The enchanted castle in Beauty and the Beast adds mystery and wonder to the story.

Prompt Exercise: Identify Story Elements

Excerpt:

Sarah gripped the worn skateboard, its paint chipped and scratched from countless adventures. Tonight, she planned to finally conquer the infamous "Gravity Drop," a heart-stopping ramp at the local skatepark.

What's the conflict?
- a) Sarah's fear of failing
- b) Conquering the "Gravity Drop"
- c) Both a and b
- d) None of the above

Correct Answer: c) Both a and b. The conflict involves Sarah's internal fears and the external challenge.

What might the theme be?
- a) Overcoming fears leads to personal growth
- b) The dangers of skateboarding
- c) Friendship is the ultimate reward
- d) Adventure is overrated

Correct Answer: a) Overcoming fears leads to personal growth.

Creating Characters that Rule

Characters are the heart and soul of your story. They're the ones who make readers laugh, cry, and cheer them on.

How to Create Memorable Characters

Key Element	Example
Give them depth	Bilbo Baggins (The Hobbit): A timid hobbit who discovers his bravery.
Show, don't tell	Instead of saying "Emma was shy," show her avoiding eye contact and speaking softly.
Unique traits	Sherlock Holmes's deductive reasoning or Hermione Granger's encyclopedic knowledge.

Prompt Exercise: Character Interaction

Prompt: Write a dialogue between two characters with clashing beliefs.

Example:
Character A: "Video games teach history in ways books never could – you get to experience events firsthand."

Character B: "But games can't replace the depth and detail you get from a textbook!"

What does this dialogue reveal about Character A?
1. *a) They value interactive learning*
2. *b) They dislike books*
3. *c) They think history is boring*
4. *d) They prefer modern approaches to education*

Correct Answer: a) They value interactive learning.

What does this reveal about Character B?
1. a) They believe in traditional learning methods
2. b) They dislike video games
3. c) They don't care about history
4. d) They value in-person classes

Correct Answer: a) They believe in traditional learning methods.

Structuring Your Story for Success

Just like a building needs a strong foundation, your story needs a solid structure to keep readers engaged.

The Plot Arc

Plot Stage	Purpose	Example
Beginning	Introduce characters, setting, and the conflict.	Frodo inherits the One Ring (The Lord of the Rings).
Rising Action	Build tension and challenges.	Frodo faces enemies on his way to Mordor.
Climax	The story's turning point.	Frodo confronts Gollum at Mount Doom.
Resolution	Tie up loose ends and show outcomes.	The ring is destroyed, and peace is restored to Middle-earth.

Prompt Exercise: Create a Story Outline

Prompt: A group of friends discover a hidden message in the school library that leads them on a treasure hunt.

Plot Stage	Your Story Ideas
Beginning	The friends find a message hidden in an old book at the library.
Rising Action	They solve riddles that take them to various landmarks in their town, each presenting new challenges.
Climax	They uncover the treasure hidden in an unexpected place.
Resolution	They share the treasure and reflect on the teamwork that brought them together.

Visual Aid: The Hero's Journey

Include a diagram showcasing The Hero's Journey, highlighting stages like:
1. Call to Adventure: The hero is introduced to their main challenge.
2. Tests and Trials: The hero faces obstacles and grows.
3. Return with Reward: The hero resolves the conflict and gains wisdom.

Creative Storytelling Examples

Story Element	Example	Key Takeaway
Plot	Harry Potter discovers he's a wizard and must face Voldemort, who killed his parents.	A strong plot combines personal stakes with an overarching conflict to keep readers engaged.
Character	Katniss Everdeen volunteers to take her sister's place in The Hunger Games.	Relatable, selfless actions make characters memorable and inspire readers to root for them.
Conflict	Frodo must destroy the One Ring before it corrupts him and falls into Sauron's hands (The Lord of the Rings).	Compelling conflicts drive the story forward and reveal a character's true strength or weakness.
Setting	The eerie, gothic mansion in Jane Eyre reflects the dark secrets hidden within.	A vivid setting enhances the mood and complements the story's tone.
Theme	In Wonder, the theme of kindness shows how compassion can transform lives.	Themes give stories depth and provide readers with meaningful lessons or reflections.
Dialogue	"I am your father." (Star Wars)	Impactful dialogue can reveal character relationships and deliver shocking twists.
Structure	The Hero's Journey in The Lion King follows Simba's growth from exile to reclaiming his kingdom.	Classic structures guide readers through a satisfying narrative arc.
Climax	Elizabeth Bennet and Mr. Darcy finally confess their feelings in Pride and Prejudice.	A well-executed climax provides the emotional payoff for your story's buildup.
Resolution	In The Fault in Our Stars, Hazel Grace finds peace in her memories of Augustus.	A resolution ties up loose ends and leaves readers with a sense of closure.
Symbolism	The green light in The Great Gatsby symbolizes Gatsby's unattainable dream.	Symbolism adds layers of meaning to the story, making it more thought-provoking.
Foreshadowing	The storm in Julius Caesar hints at the chaos that follows Caesar's assassination.	Foreshadowing builds suspense by giving subtle hints of what's to come.
Tone	The playful tone in Charlie and the Chocolate Factory contrasts with its darker themes of greed.	A story's tone sets the emotional backdrop and influences how readers interpret the events.
Perspective	The first-person narration in The Catcher in the Rye immerses readers in Holden's mindset.	Perspective shapes how the audience relates to the characters and events in the story.
Mood	The chilling mood in Dracula keeps readers on edge as they delve into the dark, mysterious world.	Mood evokes emotional responses, enhancing the reader's engagement with the story.

Trivia Corner

The Oldest Story
- The Epic of Gilgamesh, dating back over 4,000 years, is considered one of the oldest known stories. It explores timeless themes like friendship, mortality, and heroism, showcasing the enduring power of storytelling.

Character Depth
- Sherlock Holmes, the iconic fictional detective, was inspired by Dr. Joseph Bell, a real-life professor known for his sharp observational skills and ability to deduce details about people from minor clues.

Conflict in History
- The concept of "man vs. machine" as a narrative conflict emerged during the Industrial Revolution, reflecting societal fears about the impact of advancing technology on human lives and jobs.

Settings Matter
- J.R.R. Tolkien's detailed maps of Middle-earth played a vital role in shaping The Lord of the Rings, demonstrating how creating vivid settings enhances the atmosphere and depth of a story.

Themes Shape Stories
- Dr. Seuss wrote The Lorax to raise awareness about environmental conservation, making it one of the first children's books to address significant social and environmental issues.

Dialogue's Power
- Ernest Hemingway's short story Hills Like White Elephants skillfully uses sparse dialogue to reveal complex emotions and underlying tensions, illustrating the power of "show, don't tell" in storytelling.

Story Structures
- The "three-act structure" (beginning, rising action, climax, falling action, resolution) widely used in films and literature, has its roots in Aristotle's ancient theories on storytelling and drama.

Symbolism's Role
- In Nathaniel Hawthorne's The Scarlet Letter, the letter "A" represents more than adultery; it symbolizes shame, isolation, and the potential for redemption, highlighting how symbols can carry layered meanings.

Twist Endings
- O. Henry, famous for his twist endings, masterfully crafted The Gift of the Magi, where a couple's selfless sacrifices lead to an ironic yet heartwarming conclusion about love and giving.

Relatable Themes
- Pixar's stories, such as Finding Nemo and Up, resonate with audiences of all ages by exploring universal themes like family, perseverance, and loss, proving that relatable themes create lasting connections.

🎯 ACTIVITY CORNER 5

Activity 1: Identify Story Elements

Prompt: Read the following excerpt and identify the plot, conflict, and theme:

Excerpt:
Lila was thrilled to finally perform her violin solo at the school's annual concert. As she began, the power went out, leaving the auditorium in complete darkness. Undeterred, she decided to continue playing, letting the music guide her audience in the silent night.

Questions:

(1) What is the plot of this story?
  1. a) Lila's nervousness before the concert
  2. b) Lila's decision to perform despite a blackout
  3. c) The power going out during Lila's solo
  4. d) The school concert being canceled

(2) What is the theme of this story?
  1. a) The importance of practice
  2. b) Overcoming challenges through resilience
  3. c) The role of music in life
  4. d) Handling failure gracefully

Activity 2: Dialogue Creation

Prompt: Write a short dialogue between two characters with opposing views on the use of AI in storytelling.

Scenario:
Character A believes AI can enhance creativity and storytelling.
Character B feels that AI takes away originality and human touch.

Questions:

(1) Which line best reflects Character A's viewpoint?
  1. a) "AI can't replicate human emotions."
  2. b) "AI tools can help writers brainstorm and refine ideas."
  3. c) "Stories should always be written by humans."
  4. d) "Technology is a distraction for storytellers."

Questions:

(2) Which line best reflects Character B's viewpoint?
1. a) "AI-generated content can feel cold and lifeless."
2. b) "AI helps people explore storytelling possibilities."
3. c) "AI creates opportunities for new genres."
4. d) "AI is just another tool like a typewriter."

Activity 3:   Build a Story Outline

Based on the following prompt, organize a story into four parts: beginning, rising action, climax, and resolution.

Prompt: A teenager invents a device that allows them to speak to animals, leading to unexpected adventures.

Questions:

(1) What could the rising action include?

1. a) The teenager struggling to invent the device
2. b) The teenager discovering animals' unique personalities
3. c) The device malfunctioning in a critical moment
4. d) The teenager becoming famous

(2) What would make a compelling climax?

1. a) Animals stop trusting the teenager
2. b) The teenager saves the town with help from animals
3. c) The teenager learns to communicate without the device
4. d) The device becomes popular globally

6. Creative Writing for the Future

Creative Writing for the Future: Embrace Innovation and Captivate Audiences

The world is changing rapidly, and the way we communicate is transforming right along with it. Creative writing has always been a powerful tool for expressing ourselves, but today, it's more dynamic than ever before. In this chapter, we'll dive into the exciting future of writing, where you'll explore various mediums beyond pen and paper! Get ready to unleash your creativity and learn how to tell stories in fresh, captivating ways.

Introduction: Writing for Tomorrow's World

Imagine a world where stories come alive with moving images, sound effects, and interactive choices. That's the future of creative writing! As technology becomes more integrated into our lives, it's crucial to develop skills that will prepare you for the careers of tomorrow. This chapter equips you with the tools to become a future-ready writer who can:

- Craft engaging content for digital platforms like YouTube, Instagram, and TikTok.
- Design interactive stories where readers influence the plot.
- Write compelling scripts for podcasts and video content.
- And so much more!

Digital Storytelling: Captivate Your Audience Across Platforms

What is it? Digital storytelling involves weaving text, images, audio, and video to create immersive narratives. It's perfect for short-attention-span audiences who crave engaging content.

Why is it important? In today's digital age, visual content reigns supreme. By mastering digital storytelling, you can:

- Reach broader audiences across various platforms.
- Make your stories come alive with multimedia elements.
- Engage readers in innovative ways.

- **Example in Action:** Imagine a short horror story told through a YouTube video. Spooky visuals, sound effects, and narration combine to create a chilling experience, far more effective than just written text.

Your Turn! Get Creative!

- *Storyboard a 2-minute video where you narrate a personal experience. Think about visuals, audio, and transitions that could enhance your story.*

Here is one example for you:

Title: "The Day I Conquered My Fear"

Scene 1 (0-15 seconds)
- *Visual: A quick montage of images: a nervous face, a rollercoaster, a Ferris wheel, a close-up of hands gripping a railing.*
- *Audio: Upbeat, suspenseful music starts playing.*
- *Text: "Conquering Fear" appears on screen.*

Scene 2 (15-45 seconds)
- *Visual: A shot of a teenage girl (you) looking apprehensive at the entrance to an amusement park.*
- *Audio: Voiceover: "I've always been terrified of rollercoasters. The drops, the loops, the sheer speed... it all made my stomach churn."*
- *Transition: Quick cuts between shots of the girl looking nervous and shots of the rollercoaster.*

Scene 3 (45 seconds - 1 minute 15 seconds)
- *Visual: Shots of the girl actually riding the rollercoaster. Focus on close-ups of her face expressing fear and then exhilaration.*
- *Audio: Voiceover: "But my best friend, Emily, really wanted to ride the 'Viper,' the park's most terrifying rollercoaster. So, I decided to face my fear and do it with her."*
- *Audio: The sound of the rollercoaster: screams, wind, and the clicking of the track.*

Scene 4 (1 minute 15 seconds - 1 minute 45 seconds)
- *Visual: Shots of the girl and her friend laughing and celebrating after the ride.*
- *Audio: Voiceover: "It was terrifying at first, but then... I felt free! The wind in my hair, the rush of adrenaline... it was amazing."*
- *Transition: Slow-motion shot of the girl smiling.*

Scene 5 (1 minute 45 seconds - 2 minutes)
- *Visual: The girl looking at the camera, smiling.*
- *Audio: Voiceover: "That day, I learned that facing your fears can be scary, but it can also be incredibly rewarding. Sometimes, the scariest things turn out to be the most exhilarating."*
- *Text: "Conquer Your Fears!" appears on screen.*
- *Audio: Music fades out.*

Deep Dive: The Building Blocks of Digital Storytelling

Component	Description	Example
Text	The written part of your story that drives the narrative.	Narration or on-screen text.
Images	Visuals that complement or illustrate your story.	Photos, animations, or illustrations.
Audio	Sound effects, music, or voiceovers that enhance the atmosphere.	Background music, sound effects, or narration.
Video	Moving images that deliver the story's events in real-time.	Short film clips or animation.

Interactive Fiction: Where Readers Take Control

What is it? Interactive fiction (IF) lets readers become active participants in the story. By making choices, they impact the outcome, making the experience truly their own. Think video games, "Choose Your Own Adventure" books, or online stories.

Why is it important? Interactive fiction empowers readers and encourages critical thinking and problem-solving skills – essential for the digital age!

Example in Action: Imagine a "Choose Your Own Adventure" book where you decide whether a character escapes a haunted house by climbing a rope or using a secret passage. Each choice leads to a different adventure!

Challenge Yourself!

- Write a short story with three different paths for the reader.
- Include at least two possible endings based on the reader's choices.

Ready to Experiment? Explore these Tools:

- **Twine**: A free program to create interactive, non-linear stories.
- **Choice Script**: A scripting language specifically designed for interactive novels.

Blogging and Microblogging: Share Your Voice with the World

What is it? Blogging allows you to write in-depth content on a website or platform, while microblogging involves short, frequent posts on social media (think Twitter or Instagram).

Why is it important? Blogging and microblogging are powerful tools for personal branding, sharing ideas, and building an online presence. In today's job market, strong communication skills and the ability to engage audiences online are highly sought-after qualities.

Put Your Skills to the Test!

- Write a 200-word blog post about a cause you care about.
- Craft a captivating microblog post (under 150 characters) for Twitter or Instagram.

Feature	Blog	Microblog
Length	Long-form (500-1000+ words)	Short-form (less than 200 characters)
Platform	Websites like WordPress or Medium	Twitter, Instagram

Scriptwriting for Video Content: Bring Your Stories to Life on Screen

What is it?
Scriptwriting for video involves crafting engaging scripts specifically for platforms like YouTube, TikTok, or podcasts. These scripts are concise, impactful, and often include visual cues and instructions for the presenter.

Why is it important?
Video content reigns supreme today! Learning to write effective scripts for video is a valuable skill for many careers, from digital marketing and entertainment to education and even journalism.

Example in Action: A 60-second YouTube tutorial on a baking technique. The script would be concise, include clear instructions, and might even include visual cues like "Show close-up of hands mixing ingredients."

Your Turn!
- Write a one-minute script for a short tutorial or a fun, creative topic that you'd love to share with the world.

Flash Fiction and Microfiction: Tell Powerful Stories in a Nutshell

What is it?
Flash fiction is a very short story, usually under 1,000 words. Microfiction takes it even further, often with stories under 100 words. These forms challenge you to be creative and concise, focusing on plot, characters, and theme in a limited space.

Why is it important?
Flash fiction and microfiction help you hone your storytelling skills by forcing you to be economical with your words. It's a great way to practice creating impactful narratives with limited space.

Example in Action:
- **Microfiction**: "For sale: baby shoes, never worn." – Ernest Hemingway. This six-word story encapsulates a tragic tale of loss with incredible power.

Challenge Yourself!
- Write a microfiction story (under 100 words) that takes place in a futuristic or dystopian world.

Visual Poetry: Where Words Take Shape

What is it? Visual poetry combines the written word with visual art. The shape and arrangement of the words on the page become part of the poem's meaning or theme.

Why is it important?
Visual poetry pushes the boundaries of creative expression, blending writing and visual art. It's a fantastic way to explore the interplay between words and images.

Example in Action:
A poem about a tree might be shaped like a tree itself, using the branches of the text to represent the tree's limbs.

Your Turn!
- Write a poem about a theme (e.g., love, nature, time) and shape the text to form an object related to that theme (e.g., a heart for love, a leaf for nature).

Collaborative Writing: The Power of Teamwork

What is it? Collaborative writing involves working with others to create a story together. You can work online or in person, sharing ideas and combining your unique perspectives.

Why is it important? Collaborative writing fosters teamwork, communication, and idea sharing – essential skills in today's world.

Example in Action: A group of friends co-write a short story, with each person contributing a different character or part of the plot.

Challenge Yourself!
- Work with a partner to create a short story about a shared topic. Divide the writing into sections and then combine them into one cohesive narrative.

Podcast Storytelling: Bring Your Stories to Life Through Sound

What is it?
Podcast storytelling involves writing scripts specifically for audio. These can range from dramatic narratives to comedic sketches, engaging listeners through voice acting, sound effects, and music.

Why is it important? Podcasts are a hugely popular medium for storytelling. Learning to write for podcasts teaches you how to create compelling narratives using only sound.

Your Turn!
- Write a 500-word script for a podcast episode on a futuristic theme (e.g., life on Mars, AI taking over the world). Include descriptions for sound effects and background music.

Environmental Storytelling: Connecting with Nature Through Narrative

What is it? Environmental storytelling uses narrative elements to highlight environmental issues, such as climate change, sustainability, and the human-nature relationship.

Why is it important? These stories can raise awareness about critical environmental issues and inspire action.

Example in Action: A story about a small community facing the challenges of rising sea levels, highlighting the impact of climate change on human lives.

Challenge Yourself!
- Write a short story set in a world where humans and nature coexist peacefully, or one where they are in conflict over resources.

AI-Enhanced Writing: Unleash Your Creativity

- **What it is:** AI tools like ChatGPT help brainstorm, generate ideas, and refine your writing.
- **Why it matters:** Enhance your skills, boost productivity, and stay ahead in the evolving writing landscape.

Your Turn:

- **Use ChatGPT/Gemini:** Generate a short story plot outline (e.g., "AI with emotions").
- **Analyze:** Identify key elements: character, conflict, theme.

- **Expand:** Add your unique twists, character development, and vivid details to the AI-generated outline.

Key takeaway: AI is a tool to assist, not replace, your creativity.

Conclusion: The Future of Writing is Now!

The future of writing is exciting and full of possibilities. By exploring these innovative forms of storytelling, you'll not only enhance your creativity but also develop valuable skills that will prepare you for success in the digital age. So, embrace the future, experiment, and let your imagination soar!

Form	What It Is	Example	Challenge
Digital Storytelling	Multimedia narratives using text, audio, video.	A horror story told through YouTube.	Storyboard a 2-min video with visuals and audio.
Interactive Fiction	Stories with reader choices influencing outcomes.	A "Choose Your Own Adventure" story.	Write a story with 3 paths and 2 endings using Twine.
Blogging	Writing blogs or short social media updates.	Blog on climate change, Instagram post.	Write a 200-word blog and 150-character post.
Scriptwriting	Scripts for YouTube or TikTok videos.	A 60-sec baking tutorial script.	Write a 1-min tutorial script.
Flash Fiction	Stories under 1,000 or even 100 words.	Hemingway's six-word story.	Write a microfiction under 100 words.
Visual Poetry	Poetry shaped like its theme.	A tree-shaped poem on growth.	Create a visual poem shaped like a related object.
Collaborative Writing	Co-writing with others.	Group project with shared characters.	Co-write a short story with a partner.
Podcast Storytelling	Scripts for audio-based narratives.	Podcast script on life on Mars.	Write a 500-word futuristic podcast script with sound effects.
Environmental Stories	Narratives on environmental themes.	Story of a community adapting to change.	Write a story on humans and nature coexisting or in conflict.
AI-Enhanced Writing	Using AI for brainstorming or refining.	AI-generated plot turned into a story.	Use AI to create an outline and complete a story.

Trivia Corner

- *Shortest Story: Hemingway's "For sale: baby shoes, never worn" - a 6-word masterpiece of flash fiction.*

- *First Blog: "Weblog" coined in 1997; Jorn Barger created the first recognized blog.*

- *Oldest Scripts: Sumerians used cuneiform for storytelling in 3100 BCE.*
- *Interactive Fiction Roots: Emerged in the 1970s with text-based games like Zork.*

- *Digital Storytelling Pioneer: "My Hiroshima" (1990) by Kazuko Kurahara, a groundbreaking blend of narrative and multimedia.*

- *Poetry Shapes: Ancient Greeks used visual poetry techniques as early as 300 BCE.*

- *Most-Watched Script: Friends finale (52.5 million viewers) demonstrates the power of scripted storytelling.*

- *Podcast Explosion: Launched in 2004 with IT Conversations; today, over 5 million podcasts exist.*

- *Collaborative Fiction Firsts: Mary Shelley's "Frankenstein" born from a summer of ghost story collaboration in 1816.*

- *AI's Role in Writing: The Guardian published a GPT-3-written article in 2020, showcasing AI's storytelling potential.*

- *Grimm Brothers' Impact: The Grimm brothers, famous for collecting fairy tales, were also linguists and scholars, contributing significantly to the study of folklore and German language.*

ACTIVITY CORNER 6

Activity 1: Multiple Choice - Exploring Digital Storyboarding

Question: Which element is not typically included in a digital storyboard?

A. Text describing the scene
B. Visual sketches or images
C. Details about camera angles
D. A complete movie script

Activity 2: Matching - Flash Fiction Components

Question: Match the story component to its description:

Component	Description
A. Setting	1. A brief glimpse of a world in the year 2145
B. Character	2. A young girl longing for change
C. Conflict	3. The smog covering the city and the dying tree
D. Resolution	4. The girl's hope to bring nature back

Activity 3: True/False - Visual Poetry Basics

Question: Decide whether the following statements are true or false:

1. Visual poetry arranges text to form a recognizable shape.
2. A visual poem about space should be written in complete sentences.
3. The shape of a rocket is suitable for a poem on space exploration.

ACTIVITY CORNER 6

Activity 4 : Multiple Choice - Podcast Script Features

Question: Which of the following is the most important feature of a good podcast script?
A. A formal tone and lengthy details
B. Clear structure and engaging language
C. Minimalist design with no introduction
D. Repetition of key points without variety

Activity 5 : Sentence Sequencing - Storyboarding Process

Question: Arrange the following steps in the correct sequence for creating a digital storyboard:

1. Add notes for each frame.
2. Draft the key visuals or sketches.
3. Identify the scenes to be included.
4. Finalize the digital storyboard using software.

Activity 6 : Match the Pair - Elements of Interactive Fiction

Question: Match the interactive fiction term to its meaning:

Term	Meaning
A. Branching Choices	1. Tools that allow players to make decisions
B. Narrative Paths	2. Different storylines based on user actions
C. Decision Points	3. Key moments where the user selects the next action
D. Dynamic Elements	4. Features that change based on user interaction

7. Copywriting Essentials: Writing for the Digital Age

Introduction :

In today's fast-paced digital world, the ability to craft compelling and persuasive messages is crucial. Whether you're aiming to sell a product, promote a cause, or simply share an idea, effective copywriting is the key to capturing attention and driving results. This chapter explores the fundamentals of copywriting, equipping you with the skills to write persuasive and engaging content for various platforms.

What is Copywriting?

Copywriting is the art and science of writing text designed to persuade, inform, or inspire action. It is used extensively in advertising, marketing, and communication.

Key Features:

- **Purpose:** Encourage the audience to take specific actions (e.g., buy, subscribe, click).
- **Platforms**: Includes social media, websites, emails, ads, and more.

Platform	Example
Social Media	"Indulge your senses with our new summer collection! Shop now for exclusive discounts."
Advertisements	"Tired of feeling sluggish? Boost your energy with our all-natural energy drink. Try it today!"
Emails	"Urgent: Limited-time offer! Get 20% off your first order when you sign up for our newsletter."
Websites	"Experience the future of travel with our personalized vacation planning service. Book your dream trip today!"

Key Principles of Effective Copywriting

Principles and Examples

Principle	Description	Example
Attention-Grabbing Headline	The first impression that captures interest immediately.	"Unlock Your Inner Potential: 5 Steps to Achieve Your Goals"
Clear and Concise Messaging	Avoid cluttered or confusing language to maintain readability.	"Transform your workspace with our sleek and modern desks."
Know Your Audience	Tailor the tone, style, and content to match the preferences of your target readers.	Casual tone for teenagers, professional tone for business executives.
Call to Action (CTA)	Clearly direct the audience to the next step.	"Sign up now and get your first month free!"

Exercise: Identify the Best Headline

Choose the most effective headline for a fitness app:

1. "Download Our App for Fitness Goals"
2. "Achieve Your Fitness Goals Faster!"
3. "Start Your Fitness Journey Today with Expert Tips!"

Copywriting Techniques and Practice

Popular Techniques

Technique	Explanation	Example
AIDA Formula	Attention, Interest, Desire, Action - a roadmap for persuasive writing.	"Tired of feeling stuck? Discover 3 Simple Steps to Boost Your Creativity."

Technique	Explanation	Example
PAS Technique	Problem, Agitation, Solution - addressing issues and offering solutions.	"Struggling to stay organized? Our planner makes productivity simple."
Power Words	Words that evoke strong emotions and drive action.	"Unlock," "Exclusive," "Boost," "Limited."
Storytelling	Relating through a personal or emotional story.	"Imagine walking into your dream home, beautifully furnished and cozy."

Activity Corner: Create Your Own Copy

Write a persuasive post to encourage classmates to join a club or event. Include:
1. A catchy headline
2. Key benefits of joining
3. A compelling call to action

How Copywriting Prepares You for the Future

Real-World Applications

Skill	Application
Entrepreneurship	Marketing products, building a brand, and creating engaging pitches.
Digital Marketing	Managing social media accounts, creating ad campaigns, and optimizing content for search engines (SEO).
Content Creation	Writing blogs, articles, and social posts to build a personal or professional online presence.
Career Readiness	Copywriting improves critical thinking and communication, valuable in any professional setting.

An example of recent copywriting targeted at high schoolers that worked effectively is **Nike's "Play New" campaign.**

Why It Worked:

Relatability

The campaign encouraged high schoolers to explore sports and physical activities with a message of inclusivity and imperfection. It focused on the idea that it's okay to be a beginner, resonating with teens who may feel intimidated by traditional sports narratives.
Example: "Forget being the best. Just try it. Play new."

Social Media Integration:

Nike used short, engaging videos on TikTok and Instagram featuring teens and young athletes trying new activities, like yoga or skateboarding, often humorously failing before succeeding. This approach felt genuine and fun**.**

Call to Action (CTA):

Phrases like "Tag us when you try something new" and "Show us your first time trying" encouraged user-generated content, making teens feel part of a larger community.

Interactive Engagement:

Nike included challenges, such as encouraging teens to post their "first attempts" at a sport or skill, rewarding participants with shoutouts or limited-edition gear.

Emotional Appeal:

The campaign's focus on overcoming fears and celebrating small wins made it emotionally resonant. Teens, often navigating personal growth and identity, connected with the message of embracing failure as part of learning.

Trivia Corner

One of the First Print Ads
- One of the earliest known print advertisements appeared in 1477, promoting a book of prayers printed in England by William Caxton.

The Story Behind "Just Do It"
- The origin of Nike's "Just Do It" slogan is debated. While the phrase has been linked to the last words of a death-row inmate, Nike has not officially confirmed this origin story.

The AIDA Formula's Longevity
- The AIDA formula (Attention, Interest, Desire, Action) was introduced in 1898 by Elias St. Elmo Lewis, a pioneer in modern advertising, making it over 120 years old today.

The Power of "You"
- Using the word "you" in copywriting can significantly increase reader engagement by creating a sense of direct conversation and personalization.

Emotional Language Drives Action
- Advertisements with emotional language are often more effective in driving action than those relying solely on logic. They evoke stronger connections with consumers and motivate them to take action.

A Famous Six-Word Advertisement
- A six-word advertisement, "For sale: baby shoes, never worn," is often attributed to Ernest Hemingway and is considered a powerful example of brevity in storytelling.

The Impact of Red in CTAs
- Red is often used for CTAs as it can trigger urgency and excitement. Studies show red CTAs can sometimes increase conversion rates, though the impact varies based on the audience and context.

The Effectiveness of Personalization
- Personalized email subject lines can increase open rates by up to 26%, demonstrating the importance of personalization in modern copywriting.

The $200 Million Button
- A well-known anecdote suggests that Google increased revenue by $200 million by changing their CTA button text from "Book a Room" to "Check Availability," highlighting the importance of small tweaks in copywriting.

A Luxurious Commercial
- The 2004 Chanel No. 5 ad featuring Nicole Kidman was one of the most expensive commercials ever produced, with an estimated cost of $33 million.

ACTIVITY CORNER 7

Activity 1: Multiple Choice Questions

Choose the correct answer for each question.

1) What is the primary goal of copywriting?
a) Entertain the audience
b) Persuade the audience to take action
c) Provide detailed information about a topic
d) Write as much text as possible

2) Which formula is commonly used in copywriting to structure persuasive content?
a) SWOT
b) AIDA
c) PAST
d) SPAM

3) What does the word "you" in copywriting primarily achieve?
a) Fills extra space in text
b) Creates a direct, personal connection with the reader
c) Makes the writing more complex
d) None of the above

4) Which color is often used for Call-to-Action buttons to convey urgency?
a) Blue
b) Green
c) Red
d) Yellow

5) What is an example of a Call-to-Action (CTA)?
a) "Learn how to bake"
b) "Start your free trial today!"
c) "History is fascinating"
d) "Let's explore new topics together"

 ACTIVITY CORNER 7

Activity 2: Match the Following

Instructions: Match the terms in Column A with their definitions or examples in Column B.

Column A	Column B
1. Call-to-Action (CTA)	a) "For sale: baby shoes, never worn."
2. Emotional Language	b) Attention, Interest, Desire, Action
3. AIDA Formula	c) Evokes feelings to connect with the audience emotionally
4. Personalization	d) "Sign up now and get 50% off!"
5. Storytelling	e) Writing that makes the reader feel directly addressed

Activity 3 : True or False

State whether each statement is true or false.

1. Copywriting is primarily focused on providing in-depth, detailed research about topics.
2. The phrase "Just Do It" is an example of an engaging headline.
3. Emotional language is less effective in copywriting than logical arguments.
4. The AIDA formula was introduced by Elias St. Elmo Lewis in 1898.
5. Personalized subject lines in emails can increase open rates.

8. High School Writing Prompts for Creativity and Growth

Introduction: Unleashing Your Inner Writer

Writing prompts are the creative sparks that ignite your imagination and help you express yourself. They encourage exploration beyond traditional essay writing, allowing you to dive into exciting forms like screenwriting, poetry, songwriting, and blogging.

Exploring Diverse Writing Forms

Form	Description	Example
Screenwriting	Writing for film or TV, focusing on dialogue and visual storytelling.	A scene in a high school cafeteria where a student discovers a hidden talent.
Poetry	Exploring emotions, themes, and imagery in verse form.	A haiku about a sunset, a sonnet about love, or free verse about a personal experience.
Songwriting	Merging lyrical expression with rhythm and melody.	Writing a song about personal struggles, a social issue, or a fictional character.
Blogging	Writing for an online audience, focusing on personal voice and digital communication.	Starting a blog about a personal hobby, travel experiences, or social commentary.

The Power of Prompts: Igniting Imagination

How Prompts Spark Creativity

- **Overcoming Writer's Block**: Prompts help break through mental barriers. For example, if you're stuck on an essay, try a prompt like "Describe your most vivid dream" to unlock ideas.
- **Exploring Diverse Genres**: Prompts encourage experimenting with different writing styles like poetry, short stories, and screenplays. Example: "Write a short story from the perspective of a tree" challenges you to think creatively.
- **Developing Unique Voices**: Responding to varied prompts helps discover your writing style and voice. You may develop a quirky or reflective tone.
- **Building Confidence**: Successfully completing challenges boosts self-esteem and encourages taking risks with your writing.

Tips for Effective Prompt Utilization

- **Embrace the Unexpected**: Let the prompt guide you in surprising directions.
- **Experiment with Formats:**
    - Image-based Prompts: Write a story inspired by an image.
    - Scenario-driven Prompts: "What would you do if you suddenly had the power to fly?"
    - "What if" Questions: "What if the world ran out of water?"
    - Open-ended Prompts: "Write about a place you've never been but wish to visit."
- **Create Your Own Prompts:** Draw from your hobbies, interests, or questions.
- **Keep a Writing Journal**: Track your progress, reflect on responses, and identify areas for improvement.
- **Share Your Work**: Exchange your writing with peers, teachers, or online communities for feedback.

Themed Writing Prompts: Diving Deeper

Writing prompts often revolve around themes, helping students focus on specific areas while still allowing room for creativity.

Theme	Prompts
Adventure	- Write about discovering a secret passage in your school. - Imagine waking up in a different time period. - Tell the story of a mythical creature you encounter in the woods.
Personal Growth	- Describe a time you learned a difficult lesson. - Write about a personal goal you achieved and the challenges you faced. - Reflect on a childhood memory that shaped who you are today.
Mystery	- Your town loses power, and strange events begin unfolding. - You receive an anonymous letter with a cryptic message. - Investigate a series of unexplained happenings at your school.
Modern Themes	- Technology & AI: Write a story set in a world where AI writes all the books. - Social Justice: Compose a piece addressing a social issue important to you. - Environmental Concerns: Imagine how climate change impacts your community in the future.

Freewriting Challenges: Unlocking Spontaneity

Timed prompts help unlock creativity by encouraging rapid thinking and breaking the perfectionist mindset.

Timed Prompts for Spontaneous Creativity :

Challenge	Description
The 5-Minute Sprint	Write non-stop for 5 minutes about a topic or image. Encourages fluency and removes the fear of a blank page.
The 10-Minute Brainstorm	Use ten minutes to jot down as many ideas as possible related to a specific prompt. Fosters creative thinking.
The 15-Minute Story	Write a complete short story within 15 minutes. Focuses on concise writing and problem-solving.

Practice Activity:

- Write for 15 minutes about a random object in your room.
    - Example Objects: Pen, book, piece of clothing.
    - Suggested Approaches:
        - Describe the object in vivid detail.
        - Imagine its history or significance.
        - Create a story about the object—perhaps it's magical or holds a secret.

Writing Prompts in the Modern World: The Future of Creativity

Technology is reshaping how we interact with writing prompts, making the process more interactive and engaging.

The Future of Writing Prompts

Trend	Description
AI-Powered Prompts	AI algorithms generate personalized prompts, offer feedback, and suggest writing improvements.
Interactive Prompt Platforms	Online platforms integrate multimedia (images, sounds, videos) with writing prompts for an immersive experience.
Gamified Prompts	Using game mechanics (points, challenges) to make writing fun and motivating.

The Importance of Human Connection

While AI and digital tools offer exciting possibilities, the role of human feedback remains vital. Feedback from peers, teachers, and mentors adds depth and nuance to your writing journey, providing essential learning and growth opportunities.

Conclusion

Writing prompts are an essential tool for high school students, sparking creativity, honing writing skills, and fostering personal expression. Whether through traditional writing exercises or modern, tech-driven platforms, prompts unlock new perspectives, making you a more confident and versatile writer.

Trivia Corner

- The Power of "What If": "What if" questions are a classic prompt type used by writers like Ray Bradbury ("What if they tried to ban books?") to explore imaginative scenarios.

- Freewriting's Origins: Freewriting, a cornerstone of creative writing exercises, was popularized by writer and teacher Ken Macrorie in the 1960s.

- The "Six-Word Story" Challenge: Hemingway's attributed "For sale: baby shoes, never worn" sparked the popular "six-word story" challenge, encouraging concise and impactful storytelling.

- Prompt-Generating AI: Tools like GPT-3 can now generate unique and complex writing prompts, pushing creative boundaries.

- The Role of Visual Prompts: Artists like Salvador Dalí used surrealist imagery to inspire writing, demonstrating the power of visual prompts.

- Journaling as a Prompt: Daily journaling can be seen as a continuous series of self-generated prompts, encouraging reflection and self-discovery.

- The "I Am" Poem: A classic poetry prompt, the "I Am" poem encourages introspection and self-expression through a structured format.

- The "Found Poem" Technique: Creating poetry from existing texts (newspapers, song lyrics) is a unique way to repurpose language and discover hidden meanings.

- Prompt Libraries: Many online platforms and educational resources offer vast libraries of writing prompts, categorized by theme, genre, and difficulty level.

- The Impact of Social Media: Platforms like Twitter and Instagram have popularized short-form writing prompts and challenges, encouraging creative expression and online engagement.

ACTIVITY CORNER 8

Activity 1: Multiple-Choice Questions

Instructions: Match the following prompts to their genres:

Question: Match the following prompts to their genres:

1. **"Write about a dystopian future where technology rules."**
   - A. Fantasy
   - B. Science Fiction
   - C. Mystery
   - D. Historical Fiction

2. **"Describe a day in the life of your future self."**
   - A. Personal Narrative
   - B. Poetry
   - C. Adventure
   - D. Biography

Activity 2: True or False

Instructions: Determine if the following statements are true or false:

1. Freewriting involves editing as you write.
2. Open-ended prompts allow for personal interpretation.
3. Scenario-based prompts are designed to explore imaginative settings.
4. Blogging is only for professional writers.

Activity 3: Match-the-Following

Instructions: Match the type of prompt to its description:

Type of Prompt	Description
Image-Based	A. Starts with a hypothetical question to inspire creativity.
Open-Ended	B. Uses visuals to trigger imagination.
"What If" Questions	C. Encourages students to interpret in their unique way.

Activity 4: Sequencing

Question: Arrange the steps for responding to a writing prompt in the correct sequence:

A. Revise and polish your response.
B. Brainstorm ideas based on the prompt.
C. Write your first draft.
D. Choose the prompt that interests you.

Activity 5: Matching Social Media Types to Examples

Question: Match the social media type with its corresponding example:

Social Media Type	Example
Caption	An exciting moment captured: 'Life's better with friends!'
Blog Post	10 Tips for High School Success.
Tweet	Finished my latest project – can't wait to share it with you!

Activity 6: Identify the Type of Prompt

Question: Identify the type of writing prompt for each example:

1. "What if you could live underwater for a day?"
2. "Write about your favorite memory from childhood."
3. "Create a story inspired by this photograph of a busy city street."

9. Level Up Your Online Presence with Creative Writing

Why Brand Yourself Online

Think about it: college applications, future jobs – they all might involve someone checking you out online. But building an online brand isn't just about bragging rights. It's like having a digital portfolio that showcases your skills and interests.

Here's why it rocks:

- **Boss Up on Your Skills**: Running an online brand is like mini-entrepreneurship training. You'll learn about marketing, communication, and maybe even make some money!
- **Turn Your Hobbies into $$$**: Love writing, coding, or design? There are people out there who need those skills, and you can be their go-to person (and get paid for it!).
- **College and Career Ready**: Imagine a portfolio filled with your creative projects to impress colleges and potential employers. Boom!

Example:
Sarah, a 16-year-old whiz with words, created an Instagram page selling personalized poems for birthdays and holidays. Now, she's earning enough to buy that new guitar she's been eyeing. Cool, right?

Understanding Your Online Brand

Your online brand is like your digital fingerprint. It's what people see and remember about you. Here's what makes it up:

- **Your Look:** This includes your profile picture, any logos or color schemes you use. Keep it consistent across platforms. Think of it as your online outfit!

- **Your Message**: What are you passionate about? What value do you bring? Maybe you want to inspire others with your writing or help people with their coding skills.

- **Your Voice:** How do you talk (or write) online? Are you funny, informative, or super professional? Let your personality shine through!

Why Creative Writing is Your Secret Weapon

Words are powerful! Here's how creative writing can help you build a killer brand:

- **Grab Attention**: Headlines are like movie trailers for your content. Make them catchy so people stop scrolling and check out what you have to say.
- **Build Connections**: Stories tap into emotions and make people remember you. Share a personal story about overcoming writer's block or getting your first coding project to work.
- **Get People Taking Action**: A strong call to action (CTA) tells people what to do next, whether it's visiting your website, contacting you for a service, or following you for more awesome content.

Platforms to Rule the Web

- **Social Media**: Instagram is great for visuals and storytelling, while LinkedIn is more professional. Twitter is good for quick updates and connecting with like-minded people.
- **Websites or Blogs:** This is your home base where you can showcase your longer projects and creative work.
- **Marketplaces**: If you're offering services like writing or coding, sites like Fiverr can connect you with potential clients.

Crafting Your Brand Story

- **Find Your Superpower**

What are you good at? Make a list of your skills and talents. Maybe you're a whiz at writing fantasy stories, or you can code a website in your sleep. This is your starting point!

- **Write a Bio That Pops**

Here's a template to get you started:
"Hi, I'm [Your Name]. I help [Your Target Audience] with [Your Skill]. Let's connect!"
Example:
"Hi, I'm Alex! I craft epic stories that will transport you to another world. I'm also a coding wiz – hit me up if you need help with your website!"

- **Develop Your Brand Voice**

Are you chill and funny, or super professional? There's no right or wrong answer, just be you!
- **Friendly**: "Let's make your website the coolest one on the block!"
- **Professional**: "Providing high-quality content creation services."

The Art of Selling Yourself with Creative Writing

Attention-Grabbing Hooks
These are like headlines that make people stop and say, "Whoa, I gotta read that!"
- Example: "How I Went From Zero to Coding Hero (and You Can Too!)"

Storytelling
People connect with stories. Share your journey, struggles, and successes.
- Example: "From Doodling to Design: My Creative Adventure"

Compelling CTAs
Tell people what to do next!
- Example: "Click here to download my free writing guide!"

Practice Makes Perfect: Sales Post Challenge
Write a one-line social media post selling your service using a strong CTA.
Example Answer:
- "Need help writing that killer essay? I can craft compelling arguments and make your words shine. DM me for a quote!"

Selling Your Skills Online

What Can You Sell?

- Writing: Copywriting (for websites, ads, etc.)
- Storytelling
- Poetry
- Creative Writing Services (short stories, novel excerpts)
- Coding: Website Design
- App Development
- Coding Tutorials
- Art & Design: Digital Illustrations
- Graphic Design
- Custom Posters

Tips for Writing Sales Copy That Sells:

- **Focus on Benefits, Not Features:Feature:** "Custom poetry."
- **Benefit:** "Give a gift that will truly touch their heart."
- **Create a Sense of Urgency:** "Limited spots available! Book your session now."

Social Media Strategies for Creative Writers

- **X (formerly Twitter):** Share quick writing tips, industry news, and engage in relevant conversations.
- **LinkedIn:** Showcase your professional achievements, share industry insights, and connect with potential clients.
- **Instagram:** Use visuals to tell your story. Share your writing process, post inspiring quotes, and run contests.
- **TikTok**: Show off your creative process in short, engaging videos.

Scaling Your Brand

- **Collaborate**: Team up with other creators (designers, marketers, etc.) to reach a wider audience.
- **Offer Free Resources**: Attract potential clients by offering valuable freebies like writing checklists or coding tutorials.
- **Track Your Success**: Use analytics tools to see what's working and what's not. Which posts get the most likes and comments? Adjust your strategy accordingly.

Exercises: Level Up Your Online Presence

- **Write a Killer Bio:** Craft a concise and engaging bio for your LinkedIn or Instagram profile (under 150 characters).

- **The Sales Post Challenge:** Write a captivating social media post selling one of your skills.

- **Mock Campaign:** Plan a week-long social media campaign to promote a product or service you offer.

Summarizing the chapter

Section	Description	Example	Activity
Introduction	Overview of why teens should build an online brand.	A 16-year-old earns $500/month selling poetry online.	Reflect on your skills. Write down one thing you could monetize (e.g., writing, coding).
Understanding Online Branding	Explains core components of a brand and the importance of creative writing.	Visual Identity: A consistent theme on Instagram (e.g., blue visuals).	Identify your voice: Write a tagline that represents your personal brand.
Crafting Brand Identity	Steps to define skills, mission, and create an engaging bio.	"Hi, I'm Alex! I write engaging copy to boost startups' brand voice."	Write your own bio for LinkedIn, Instagram, or X.
Selling Yourself with Writing	Teaches attention-grabbing hooks, storytelling, and CTAs.	Hook: "How I turned $50 into $500 designing websites!"	Create a social media post selling a skill with a clear CTA.
Proof of Concept	Encourages testing skills by selling products or services online.	Writing: Sell custom poetry for $20 each.	List 3 skills or products you could sell. Craft a short post for one of them.
Social Media Strategies	Platform-specific strategies for creative writing and branding.	TikTok: Post videos showing how you write engaging headlines in real-time.	Draft a sample post for a platform of your choice.
Scaling Your Brand	Tips for collaboration, free resources, and analytics.	Collaborate with a designer to offer full branding packages.	Plan a collaborative idea with a classmate who has complementary skills.
Exercises and Test Cases	Activities to practice online branding and selling.	Create a week-long campaign to sell custom short stories.	Write a mock campaign post for social media, including a hook, story, and CTA.

Trivia Corner

Trivia Facts: Creative Writing and Online Branding

Young Entrepreneurs in Action
- Moziah Bridges, a Memphis teen, launched Mo's Bows at 12, turning his passion for bow ties into a successful business. His creative storytelling, including his appearance on Shark Tank, played a crucial role in building his brand.

Virality Can Be Unexpected
- The phrase "OK Boomer" unexpectedly exploded in popularity after a TikTok video. This viral phenomenon demonstrates how online trends can quickly evolve into business opportunities, as seen in the merchandise that capitalized on the phrase.

The Power of Personal Connection
- Studies show that social media posts with personal stories receive 22% higher engagement than purely factual ones. This highlights the importance of human connection and authenticity in online branding.

Teen-Driven Innovation
- Ben Pasternak, a young entrepreneur, developed the Flogg app for selling used items. His creative pitch and innovative idea attracted significant funding, emphasizing the power of compelling storytelling in attracting investment.

The Rise of Micro-Influencers
- Micro-influencers (with 1,000-10,000 followers) often have higher engagement rates than celebrities. High school students can leverage this by authentically showcasing their skills to a targeted audience.

The $5 Side Hustle
- Fiverr, a popular freelancing platform, began with services priced at just $5. It has since grown significantly, with teenagers actively participating in the gig economy by offering services like writing, design, and coding.

Stories Sell Better
- Instagram posts with story-like captions (e.g., "I struggled with X, then discovered Y") outperform simple descriptions by 37%. This emphasizes the power of narrative in capturing audience attention and engagement.

Trivia Corner

Fastest Instagram Growth
- Khabane Lame became the most-followed person on Instagram in 2022 without speaking a single word. His creative use of simple, relatable content demonstrates the power of visual storytelling and humor in building a massive online following.

Digital Writing is the Future
- By 2030, it's estimated that 75% of jobs will require strong digital writing and communication skills. This makes online branding and effective digital communication increasingly essential for career success.

Teen Titans of Branding
- Emma Chamberlain, a YouTube influencer, successfully launched Chamberlain Coffee at a young age. Her unique online persona and creative branding strategies effectively engaged a large audience and built a successful coffee brand.

The 280-Character Revolution
- Twitter (now X) increased its character limit from 140 to 280 in 2017. Studies show that tweets with fewer than 140 characters still perform better, proving that concise creative writing is a powerful tool for engagement.

Teen Millionaires from Dropshipping
- A high school student, Isabella Barrett, started a dropshipping business at age 14 by branding herself as a fashion influencer. She combined social media storytelling and creative writing to grow her business into a multimillion-dollar empire.

Creative Slogans Stick
- The Nike slogan "Just Do It" was inspired by the last words of a criminal but became one of the most successful brand taglines. This highlights how unusual sources of inspiration can create memorable branding.

ACTIVITY CORNER 9

Activity 1: Match the Platform with the Strategy

Instructions: Match the social media platform with the most suitable creative writing strategy.

Platforms	Strategies
1. Instagram	A. Use concise, professional tone and list achievements.
2. LinkedIn	B. Share personal stories with visual storytelling.
3. X (formerly Twitter)	C. Leverage short, witty updates or trending hashtags.
4. TikTok	D. Use captions that complement short, engaging videos.
5. Facebook	E. Write longer posts with relatable storytelling.

Activity 2 : Match the Prompt with the Tagline

Instructions: Match each prompt with the most suitable tagline for marketing services.

Prompts	Taglines
1. A high schooler offering graphic design	A. "Your Story, My Design – Let's Create Magic Together!"
2. A teenager writing poetry for events	B. "Engage Your Audience with Tailored Designs That Speak Volumes."
3. A coder building websites for businesses	C. "Code Your Vision, One Line at a Time."
4. A student editing videos for influencers	D. "Transforming Moments into Visual Masterpieces."
5. A writer creating personalized stories	E. "Words That Bring Your Unique Story to Life – Just for You!"

🎯 ACTIVITY CORNER 9

Activity 3 : True or False: Building Your Brand

1. Writing long paragraphs is the best way to capture attention on Instagram.
2. A CTA (Call to Action) increases the likelihood of user engagement.
3. Consistency in tone and messaging is crucial for building a recognizable brand.
4. Creative storytelling is irrelevant when marketing technical skills like coding.
5. High school students cannot start selling services like copywriting online.

Activity 4 : Multiple-Choice Questions

1. **What is the primary goal of creative writing in building an online brand?**
   - A. To showcase your vocabulary
   - B. To connect emotionally with your target audience
   - C. To write lengthy descriptions about yourself
   - D. To avoid using visuals in your posts

2. **Which of the following best describes a strong call-to-action (CTA) in a social media post?**
   - A. "Hope you liked it!"
   - B. "Click the link to start your journey today!"
   - C. "Just writing my thoughts, no big deal."
   - D. "Check it out, or don't—it's up to you."

3. **What is an essential element of a successful personal brand tagline?**
   - A. It uses technical jargon to impress your audience.
   - B. It is vague and open to interpretation.
   - C. It is concise, memorable, and reflects your value proposition.
   - D. It is long and detailed to ensure clarity.

4. **What platform is ideal for showcasing your coding or web design skills through creative writing?**
   A. Instagram
   B. LinkedIn
   C. TikTok
   D. Pinterest

10. Creative Writing for the Digital Age: Modern Applications and Exercises

"In our hyper-connected world, creative writing transcends novels and essays. It's the engine of digital communication, powering everything from captivating tweets to immersive brand stories.

This chapter equips high school students with the skills to excel in this dynamic landscape. We'll explore 10 key areas, providing practical exercises to master the art of crafting compelling content for the digital age – a skillset crucial for future success in fields like marketing, education, and media.

1. Tweet

Example:
You're running a campaign to encourage students to adopt eco-friendly habits.
Tweet Example:

🌱 **Small actions, BIG impact! Switch to reusable bottles and ditch plastic waste. Together, let's save the planet!** 🌍 #EcoWarrior #SustainableLiving

Exercises/Prompts:
1. *Write a tweet encouraging your classmates to join a school recycling program. Include an emoji and a hashtag.*
2. *Draft a tweet promoting a bake sale to fund a field trip. Make it engaging in 280 characters or less.*
3. *Create a tweet celebrating a recent school achievement. Use two emojis and a hashtag.*

2. LinkedIn Post

Example:
You're sharing your experience from a school leadership workshop.

LinkedIn Post Example:

"Last weekend, I had the privilege of attending the Youth Leadership Summit 2025. It was an incredible experience to learn about teamwork, problem-solving, and innovative thinking from industry leaders.

The highlight? Collaborating with peers to design solutions for real-world challenges! I'm excited to bring these skills back to my school community.

Here's to growing as a leader and making a difference! 🌟

#LeadershipSkills #YouthEmpowerment #GrowthMindset"

Exercises/Prompts:
1. Write a LinkedIn post highlighting your role in organizing a school event. Include 3 hashtags and a personal reflection.
2. Draft a post announcing your participation in a community service project. Mention key takeaways in 100–150 words.
3. Create a post celebrating a personal achievement, such as winning a debate or a sports competition, emphasizing the skills you gained.

3. Sales Page Copywriting

Example:

You're writing a sales page for a new app that helps students stay organized.

Sales Page Copy Example:

Introducing StudySmart: Your Ultimate Study Companion! 📚

Struggling to stay on top of assignments and deadlines? Say goodbye to chaos with StudySmart!

- 📅 Smart Scheduling: Plan your day effortlessly with personalized timetables.
- 📊 Progress Tracking: See your study goals and achievements at a glance.
- ⏰ Reminders That Work: Never miss a deadline again.

Why Choose StudySmart?
- Easy to use
- Designed by students, for students
- Available on all devices

📣 **Download StudySmart Today and Get a Free Trial!**

Exercises/Prompts:

- Write a sales pitch for a new eco-friendly notebook designed for students. Highlight 3 features and a special offer.
- Draft a short sales copy for an educational website subscription offering live tutorials for exam prep. Mention at least 2 benefits.
- Create an engaging sales page for a sports water bottle with a built-in filter. Include a catchy headline and bullet points for features.

4. Digital Storytelling

In the digital age, storytelling is no longer confined to books or films. Digital storytelling combines creative writing with multimedia elements like videos, images, and audio to craft compelling narratives. It allows creators to connect with audiences on an emotional level, using platforms like Instagram, TikTok, or dedicated storytelling apps. This form of writing has applications in marketing, personal branding, and even education, making it an invaluable skill for high school students.

Example: You're tasked with creating a 2-minute digital story about a school recycling initiative. Below is the script:

Title: **"A Greener Tomorrow: The School Recycling Revolution"**

- Opening Scene: [Soft background music fades in; visuals show students dropping cans into recycling bins.]
- Narrator: "What if every bottle, every can, could help change the world? Here at Lincoln High, we're making that vision a reality."
- Middle Scene: [Transition to students sorting items, statistics overlay appears on screen.]
- Narrator: "Every month, over 5,000 recyclable items are collected, saving hundreds of pounds of waste from landfills."
- Ending Scene: [Inspirational music swells, students smiling around the bins.]
- Narrator: "Join us in our journey to a greener tomorrow. One can at a time.

Exercises/Prompts:

1. Write a 1-minute Instagram story script about a school sports event, highlighting its significance.
2. Create a short TikTok script encouraging peers to volunteer for a local community cause.
3. Draft a digital story script promoting mental health awareness for teens.

5. Blogging

Blogging is a versatile form of creative writing that allows students to express ideas, share experiences, and showcase expertise. It's a powerful tool for personal branding and learning to communicate effectively in the digital space.

Example Blog Post:

Title: "The Secret to Staying Organized in High School"

Introduction:

High school can feel overwhelming with assignments, extracurricular activities, and social commitments piling up. Staying organized is the key to balancing it all and achieving your goals. In this blog, I'll share three simple strategies that helped me stay on top of my schedule and still find time for fun!

Body:

1. Use a Planner or Digital Calendar

A planner is a lifesaver when it comes to keeping track of deadlines, test dates, and events. If you prefer digital tools, apps like Google Calendar or Notion can send you reminders and help you visualize your week. Write everything down, even small tasks—this ensures you won't forget anything important.

2. Declutter Your Study Space

A messy desk leads to a cluttered mind. Take 10 minutes each week to organize your study space. Use folders for papers, label your notebooks, and keep only the essentials on your desk. A clean space can improve focus and make studying more efficient.

3. Prioritize Tasks with the 'ABC' Method

Not all tasks are equally important. Use the 'ABC' method to rank them:
- A: Must do (urgent assignments, test prep)
- B: Should do (club meeting prep, optional homework)
- C: Nice to do (browsing hobbies, socializing).
- Start with A tasks and work your way down. This way, you focus on what truly matters.

Conclusion:

Staying organized isn't as hard as it seems—it just requires a few simple habits! By using a planner, decluttering your space, and prioritizing tasks, you'll feel more in control and less stressed. Give these tips a try, and let me know how they work for you in the comments!

Exercises/Prompts:

1. Write a blog post titled "3 Ways to Make Studying Fun."
2. Draft a blog post sharing your favorite vacation experience, focusing on sensory details.
3. Create a how-to blog on organizing your study desk for maximum productivity.

6. YouTube Video Script Writing

YouTube scriptwriting combines storytelling, structure, and audience engagement. A well-crafted script ensures the video delivers its message effectively while keeping viewers entertained and informed.

Example :

Video Title: "5 Study Hacks Every High Schooler Should Know"

Script:
- Introduction: [Energetic music; host on screen.]
- Host: "Hey everyone! Studying doesn't have to be boring or stressful. Today, I'll share five awesome study hacks to make your life easier!"
- Hack 1: [Overlay visuals of color-coded notes.]
- Host: "Use color-coded notes. Assign colors for different topics—it'll help your brain retain information better."
- Hack 2: [B-roll of a timer ticking.]
- Host: "Try the Pomodoro technique. Study for 25 minutes, then take a 5-minute break. It keeps your focus sharp."
- Closing: [Host smiling, call-to-action overlay appears.]
- Host: "Which hack will you try first? Comment below and don't forget to like and subscribe for more tips!"

Exercises/Prompts:

1. Write a script for a 2-minute YouTube video about "How to Make Quick and Healthy Snacks."
2. Draft a script for a vlog about a day in your life as a high school student.
3. Create a short tutorial script explaining a science experiment using household items.

7. Gamified Content Creation

Gamification integrates game-like elements into educational, marketing, or entertainment content to engage and motivate users. Creative writing for gamified content involves designing interactive stories, challenges, and rewards that keep audiences hooked. This skill is ideal for students interested in game design, marketing, or e-learning.

Example: Write a storyline for a mobile game where players solve mysteries to progress, incorporating characters, settings, and challenges.

Game Title: "Cipher City: Secrets of the Skyline"

Storyline:
Premise: Players take on the role of "The Decoder," a newly inducted member of a secret society within their bustling metropolis – Cipher City. This society, known as "The Owls," has been tasked with maintaining the city's delicate balance of order and chaos.

Script:
- Introduction: [Energetic music; host on screen.]
- Host: "Hey everyone! Studying doesn't have to be boring or stressful. Today, I'll share five awesome study hacks to make your life easier!"
- Hack 1: [Overlay visuals of color-coded notes.]
- Host: "Use color-coded notes. Assign colors for different topics—it'll help your brain retain information better."
- Hack 2: [B-roll of a timer ticking.]
- Host: "Try the Pomodoro technique. Study for 25 minutes, then take a 5-minute break. It keeps your focus sharp."
- Closing: [Host smiling, call-to-action overlay appears.]
- Host: "Which hack will you try first? Comment below and don't forget to like and subscribe for more tips!"

Exercises/Prompts:

1. Write a script for a 2-minute YouTube video about "How to Make Quick and Healthy Snacks."
2. Draft a script for a vlog about a day in your life as a high school student.
3. Create a short tutorial script explaining a science experiment using household items.

7. Gamified Content Creation

Gamification integrates game-like elements into educational, marketing, or entertainment content to engage and motivate users. Creative writing for gamified content involves designing interactive stories, challenges, and rewards that keep audiences hooked. This skill is ideal for students interested in game design, marketing, or e-learning.

Example: Write a storyline for a mobile game where players solve mysteries to progress, incorporating characters, settings, and challenges.

Game Title: "Cipher City: Secrets of the Skyline"

Storyline:
Premise: Players take on the role of "The Decoder," a newly inducted member of a secret society within their bustling metropolis – Cipher City. This society, known as "The Owls," has been tasked with maintaining the city's delicate balance of order and chaos.

Characters:

- **The Decoder (Player):** A quick-witted and curious high school student who excels in puzzles and critical thinking.
- **Professor Onyx:** The enigmatic leader of The Owls, a wise and experienced mentor who guides the Decoder through their missions.
- **Agent Raven:** A skilled field operative and tech expert, providing crucial information and support.
- **Cipher:** A mischievous AI assistant with a sarcastic wit, who helps the Decoder navigate the digital world and decipher coded messages.

Settings:

- **Cipher City:** A vibrant metropolis with a rich history, filled with hidden passages, secret societies, and intriguing characters.
    - **The Clocktower:** The Owls' headquarters, a hidden sanctuary within a towering clocktower overlooking the city.
    - **The Museum of Curiosities:** A museum filled with strange artifacts and cryptic puzzles.
    - **The Digital District:** A futuristic tech hub where cybercrimes and data breaches occur frequently.
    - **The Old Quarter:** A historic district with ancient riddles and hidden symbols embedded in its architecture.

Challenges:

- **Puzzles:Cipher Puzzles:** Decrypting coded messages, solving anagrams, and breaking complex ciphers.
- **Logic Puzzles:** Solving riddles, identifying patterns, and piecing together clues.
- **Environmental Puzzles:** Finding hidden objects, navigating intricate mazes, and interacting with the environment.
- **Investigations:Tracking down suspects:** Following leads, interviewing witnesses, and analyzing evidence.
- **Uncovering conspiracies:** Investigating suspicious activity and uncovering hidden agendas.
- **Stopping cyberattacks:** Tracing the source of hacking attempts and preventing data breaches.

Exercises/Prompts:

1. Design a treasure hunt game with a storyline and a series of clues leading to the final prize.
2. Write a quiz-based game script that tests knowledge of a school subject with fun rewards.
3. Develop an interactive story where players make choices that shape the ending.

8. Educational Content Development

Educational content writing focuses on creating materials like lesson plans, e-books, quizzes, and videos for learning platforms. With the rise of digital education, this type of writing is a future-proof skill for students who enjoy teaching and sharing knowledge creatively.

Example: Write a script for an animated video explaining the water cycle to middle school students using simple language and visual

Compact script for an animated video explaining the water cycle to middle school students, focusing on clarity and conciseness:

(Visual: Sun shining on an ocean)
Narrator: The sun warms ocean water, turning it into invisible water vapor.
(Visual: Water vapor rising, forming clouds)
Narrator: This is evaporation. Water vapor rises, cools, and forms clouds.
(Visual: Rain falling from clouds)
Narrator: Clouds release water as rain, snow, or hail. This is precipitation.
(Visual: Rain falling on land, some soaking into the ground, some flowing into a river)
Narrator: Rainwater soaks into the ground (groundwater) or flows into rivers.
(Visual: River flowing into the ocean)
Narrator: All water eventually returns to the ocean.
(Visual: Cycle repeats)
Narrator: This continuous journey is the water cycle. It provides us with fresh water and sustains life on Earth.

Exercises/Prompts:

1. Develop a list of 10 fun facts about a science topic for an educational infographic.
2. Write a script for a 2-minute video that explains a math concept using examples.
3. Create a multiple-choice quiz for history or geography with engaging explanations for the answers.

9. Technical Writing

Technical writing focuses on clear and concise communication for manuals, user guides, and instructional content. In the digital era, technical writers are essential for software companies, tech startups, and other industries. High school students with an eye for detail can develop this skill to pursue tech-oriented careers.

Example: Write a step-by-step user guide for setting up a new smartphone, covering all key features and troubleshooting tips.

Setting Up Your New Smartphone: A Quick Guide

1. Power Up & Initial Setup:

- Charge: Plug in your phone to charge.
- Power On: Press and hold the power button.
- Language & Region: Select your preferred language and region.
- Google Account: Sign in with your existing Google Account (recommended) or create a new one. This allows you to access Google services like Gmail, Play Store, and Google Maps.
- Wi-Fi: Connect to your home Wi-Fi network for faster setup and downloads.

2. Essential Apps & Settings:

- Play Store: Download and install essential apps:
    - Social Media: Instagram, Snapchat, TikTok
    - Messaging: WhatsApp, Messenger, Textra SMS
    - Productivity: Google Maps, Calendar, Notes
    - Entertainment: Spotify, Netflix (if applicable)
    - Personalize:Home Screen: Customize your home screen with widgets, folders, and live wallpapers.
    - Lock Screen: Set a secure lock screen (password, PIN, or fingerprint).
    - Notifications: Adjust notification settings for each app to avoid distractions.

Exercises/Prompts:

1. Write instructions for assembling a piece of furniture, using clear headings and steps.
2. Create a quick-start guide for using a popular app like Zoom or Canva.
3. Develop a glossary of terms explaining key concepts for a technology-related topic.

10. Branded Storytelling

Branded storytelling blends creative writing with marketing, using narratives to build a connection between a brand and its audience. This skill is essential for students interested in advertising, public relations, or content creation for companies. It focuses on evoking emotions and building trust.

Example: Write a story about a fictional café that shows how it helps bring people together, tying the narrative to the brand's values.

The aroma of freshly brewed coffee hung heavy at "The Daily Grind," a quirky little café nestled in the heart of the bustling city. Its mismatched chairs, vintage record player, and walls adorned with local artwork whispered stories of community and connection.

One rainy afternoon, a young woman named Maya, drenched and disheartened after a job interview, stumbled into The Daily Grind. The barista, a kind soul named Ben, greeted her with a warm smile and a steaming cup of chai. As Maya sipped her chai, lost in thought, an elderly gentleman, Mr. Thompson, struck up a conversation. He shared stories of his life as a traveling musician, his voice filled with a passion that ignited a spark within Maya.

Intrigued, Maya began visiting The Daily Grind regularly. She met other regulars: a group of students collaborating on a film project, a retired teacher sharing his wisdom with aspiring writers, and a lonely artist finding solace in the café's creative atmosphere.
One day, Maya, inspired by the community she found at The Daily Grind, decided to organize a "Community Art Day" at the café. Local artists were invited to showcase their work, and the café buzzed with creativity. The event brought together people from all walks of life, fostering a sense of belonging and connection.

The Daily Grind, with its focus on community, had become more than just a café; it was a sanctuary for lost souls, a hub for creative minds, and a testament to the power of human connection.

Brand Values:

- **Community**: The café fosters a sense of community by bringing people together and creating a welcoming space for interaction.
- **Creativity**: The café supports local artists and encourages creative expression among its patrons.
- **Human Connection:** The café emphasizes the importance of human interaction and the power of meaningful conversations.

Exercises/Prompts:

1. Create a short Instagram post that tells the story of a brand's journey from idea to success.
2. Write a tagline and mini-story for a startup that focuses on eco-friendly products.
3. Develop a story-based ad script for a product aimed at teenagers, highlighting its benefits creatively.

Trivia Corner

Shortest Story in the World:
- Ernest Hemingway is often credited with writing a six-word story: "For sale: baby shoes, never worn." It's a classic example of storytelling brevity that inspires digital writers to say more with less.

The First Blog:
- The term "weblog" was coined by Jorn Barger in 1997, marking the birth of blogging. Today, over 7 million blog posts are published daily worldwide.

Rise of Short-Form Content:
- Platforms like Twitter and TikTok prioritize concise, engaging content. Twitter's original character limit of 140 characters pushed creators to innovate in brevity.

Digital Storytelling Goes Global:
- The most-watched YouTube video of all time, "Baby Shark Dance," demonstrates how digital storytelling crosses languages and cultures, amassing over 13 billion views.

Gamified Content is Everywhere:
- The use of gamified elements in marketing, like Starbucks' rewards app, has shown that interactive storytelling can boost user engagement by up to 30%.

Educational Blogs for Students:
- Blogs like Khan Academy and ThoughtCo rank among the most visited educational blogs, proving how digital content can revolutionize learning for students globally.

YouTube is the New Classroom:
- Over 86% of teenagers use YouTube as a learning tool, with creators turning complex topics into digestible, entertaining videos.

Branded Storytelling is Booming:
- Brands like Nike use storytelling to build emotional connections with their audiences, often driving campaigns that combine personal stories with digital outreach.

AI in Writing:
- AI tools like ChatGPT and Jasper are redefining how content is created, offering assistance with brainstorming, writing, and editing, making them invaluable for future careers.

Technical Writing Growth:
- The demand for technical writers has grown by 10% in the last decade as industries increasingly rely on clear, concise digital documentation.

ACTIVITY CORNER 10

Activity 1: Writing a Compelling Tweet – Multiple Choice Questions

Question 1

Which of the following tweets best includes a call-to-action?

- A. "Our school fundraiser starts tomorrow. Don't forget to participate!"
- B. "Join us in making a difference. Donate to our school fundraiser today! #EducationForAll"
- C. "We are hosting a fundraiser for our school library. Let's make it a success!"
- D. "The school library fundraiser is here. Support us if you can."

Question 2

Which tweet is most effective for engaging an audience for a new art club?

- A. "Our new art club starts next week. Join us!"
- B. "Are you passionate about art? Join our school art club and showcase your talent! 🎨 #CreativeStudents"
- C. "We have a new art club. It's going to be fun. Don't miss it!"
- D. "Art lovers, this is your chance to shine. Come to the new art club."

Question 3

Which tweet is most suitable for promoting an eco-friendly event?

- A. "Attend our event to learn about eco-friendliness!"
- B. "Be a part of the green revolution. 🌱 Join our eco-friendly event this Friday and make a difference! #GoGreen"
- C. "Our eco-friendly event is happening soon. Come join us."
- D. "Save the planet. Attend our event about eco-friendly practices."

Question 4

Which tweet effectively uses hashtags to promote a school sports day?

- A. "Sports day is here. Be there and cheer for our teams!"
- B. "Excited for sports day? Join us this Saturday and support our athletes! 🏆 #SchoolSpirit #GameOn"
- C. "Our annual sports day will be on Saturday. Come and watch."
- D. "Sports lovers, mark your calendar for Saturday's sports day."

ACTIVITY CORNER 10

Question 5

Which tweet is best for encouraging donations to a school charity drive?

- A. "We need your support for our charity drive."
- B. "Every donation counts! Help us spread kindness through our charity drive. 🖤 Donate now! #SupportCharity #MakeADifference"
- C. "Our charity drive starts tomorrow. Please donate."
- D. "Charity drive alert! We need donations to make it a success."

Activity 2: Match the Following

A	B
1. Digital Storytelling	a. A script written for a short 2-minute online video
2. Blogging	b. Writing a post on social media to encourage engagement and discussion
3. YouTube Video Script Writing	c. Crafting a compelling narrative using multimedia like text, images, audio, and video
4. Gamified Content Creation	d. Creating an interactive story where readers influence the plot
5. Educational Content Development	e. Developing instructional materials, guides, or courses aimed at teaching students or learners

Activity 3 : Fill in the Blanks

Complete the sentences with the correct terms related to digital content creation.

1. _____ involves creating stories using multimedia elements such as text, video, audio, and images to engage the audience.
2. _____ is a type of writing specifically intended to be shared online in blog posts, articles, or web content.
3. A _____ is typically written for online platforms like YouTube, guiding the visuals and dialogue throughout a video.
4. _____ is a form of interactive storytelling where the audience's choices affect the direction of the plot.
5. _____ is the process of creating learning materials or resources, often through videos, articles, or courses, to educate or inform others

ACTIVITY ANSWERS

ACTIVITY CORNER 1

1. Identify the Writing Type

1. Creative Writing
2. Informative Writing
3. Persuasive Writing
4. Analytical Writing

2. Choose the Correct Format

1. Script
2. Short Story
3. Poem
4. Personal Essay

5. Identify the Purpose

1. To persuade
2. To entertain
3. To analyze
4. To inform

3. Complete the Sentence

1. Short story
2. Meter
3. Script
4. Personal essay

4. True or False

1. False
2. True
3. False
4. True

6. Match Terms with Their Definitions

1 - d
2 - b
3 - c
4 - a

ACTIVITY CORNER 2

1) Grammar and Parts of Speech (MCQ)

1. c) Adjective
2. d) Adverb
3. c) Noun
4. a) Verb
5. b) Adjective

2. Match the Sentence Structure

1. 1 → c. The dog barked loudly.
2. 2 → b. I went to the store, and I bought some milk.
3. 3 → a. After the storm passed, we went outside to play.
4. 4 → d. When I arrived, the show had started, but I still enjoyed it.

3) Punctuation Practice

1. We visited Paris, London, and Rome during our vacation.
2. After the movie, we went to grab some dinner.
3. She loves reading, but she also enjoys painting.
4. Are you coming to the party tomorrow?
5. I can't believe it's already December!

4. Build a Paragraph

Sentence	Position (1-5)
Social media platforms like Instagram and TikTok allow users to share videos instantly.	3
Social media is a transformative tool in today's world.	1
These platforms have also become essential for businesses to reach new audiences.	4
People can connect with family and friends regardless of distance.	2
It has revolutionized the way we communicate and share ideas.	5

ACTIVITY CORNER 3

ACTIVITY 1: MULTIPLE CHOICE

Answers:
1. B
2. B
3. C
4. B
5. B

ACTIVITY 2 : MATCH THE FOLLOWING

Terms	Descriptions
A. Thesis Statement	2. The central argument of your persuasive piece
B. Logical Evidence	3. Facts, data, or statistics supporting the argument
C. Emotional Appeal	1. Using emotions to connect with the audience
D. Raise Awareness	4. A goal to bring attention to a critical issue

ACTIVITY 3 : PROMPT CHALLENGE

Prompt 1: Here's a sample paragraph persuading your school principal to extend recess time:

"Extending recess time is crucial for student well-being and academic success. Research shows that regular physical activity improves focus, attention, and cognitive function. Increased playtime allows students to release pent-up energy, reducing disruptive behavior in the classroom. Moreover, recess provides a valuable opportunity for social interaction and emotional development, fostering friendships and teamwork. Imagine a school where children are happier, healthier, and more engaged in learning – a longer recess can make this vision a reality."

- Clear Thesis Statement: "Extending recess time is crucial for student well-being and academic success."
    - **Logical Evidence**: "Research shows that regular physical activity improves focus, attention, and cognitive function."
    - "Increased playtime reduces disruptive behavior in the classroom."
    - **Emotional Appeal**: "Imagine a school where children are happier, healthier, and more engaged in learning."

This paragraph presents a concise and persuasive argument for extending recess time, effectively combining logic and emotional appeal to convince the principal.

ACTIVITY CORNER 3
ACTIVITY 3 : PROMPT CHALLENGE

Prompt 2: Here's a sample speech persuading your family to adopt a dog:

"Hi everyone, I've been thinking a lot lately about how much happier our family would be with a dog. Studies have shown that owning a pet can actually reduce stress levels and lower blood pressure, which would be great for all of us. Remember how much fun I had playing with **Leo**? I know I'd love to have a furry friend to play wit h every day. We could go for walks in the park, teach them tricks, and even take them to the dog park. I promise to help with all the responsibilities, like feeding, walking, and grooming. Having a dog would bring so much joy and laughter to our home, and I truly believe it would make us a happier and healthier family."

This speech includes:
- **Clear Benefit**: "reduce stress levels and lower blood pressure"
- **Statistic**: "Studies have shown that owning a pet can actually reduce stress levels and lower blood pressure"
- **Personal Anecdote**: "Remember how much fun I had playing with Leo [Name of dog from neighbor's house or a dog you met]?"

ACTIVITY 3 : FILL IN THE BLANKS

Answers
1. Thesis
2. Logical
3. Emotion
4. Emotional
5. Conclusion

ACTIVITY 4 : PROMPT CHALLENGE: MATCH THE FOLLOWING

Answers
1 → b (Thesis Statement: The main argument or central idea of your essay.)
2 → d (Logical Appeal: Uses facts, data, and evidence to support an argument.)
3 → e (Emotional Appeal: Evokes feelings to create a connection with the audience.)
4 → a (Anecdote: A brief personal story used to connect with the audience.)
5 → c (Call to Action: Encourages the audience to take specific steps or actions.)

ACTIVITY CORNER 4

ACTIVITY 1: ANALYZING A SOCIAL MEDIA POST

(1) Answer: b) Informative
Explanation: The post aims to share facts and encourage action in an educational way.

(2) Answer: c) Inspire action
Explanation: The purpose is to encourage recycling to reduce ocean pollution.

ACTIVITY 2: ANALYZE A COMMERCIAL OR ADVERTISEMENT

Answer Key:

(1) Answer: b) Young athletes
Explanation: The ad's focus on youth challenges and inspiration connects best with young athletes.

(2) Answer: c) Motivation
Explanation: The ad encourages determination and perseverance through inspiring visuals and messaging.

ACTIVITY 3: DISSECT A MOVIE SCENE

Answer Key:

1. Answer: b) Oppression
Explanation: The dull colors reflect the grim and oppressive reality of the characters' world.

2. Answer: a) Sacrifice for loved ones
Explanation: Katniss volunteers for her sister, highlighting the theme of personal sacrifice.

ACTIVITY 4: REWRITE AN ARGUMENT WITH BETTER EVIDENCE

Answer Key:

1. Answer: a) Uniforms create equality, reducing bullying.
Explanation: Reducing bullying is a strong, evidence-based reason for supporting school uniforms.

2. Answer: c) School uniforms create equality and reduce bullying.
Explanation: This statement is clear, focused, and supported by logical evidence.

ACTIVITY CORNER 5

Activity 1: Identify Story Elements

Answers:
1. b) Lila's decision to perform despite a blackout (the plot focuses on her response to the blackout).
2. b) Overcoming challenges through resilience (the theme highlights her determination and adaptability).

Activity 2: Dialogue Creation

Answer Key:
1. b) AI tools can help writers brainstorm and refine ideas.
2. a) AI-generated content can feel cold and lifeless.

Activity 3: Build a Story Outline

Answers:
1. b) The teenager discovering animals' unique personalities (adds excitement and builds tension).
2. b) The teenager saves the town with help from animals (a dramatic turning point).

ACTIVITY CORNER 5

Activity 1: Multiple Choice - Exploring Digital Storyboarding

Answers:
1. D. A complete movie script

Activity 2: Matching - Flash Fiction Components

Answers:
- A - 1
- B - 2
- C - 3
- D - 4

Activity 3 : True/False - Visual Poetry Basics

Answers:
1. True
2. False
3. True

Activity 4 : Multiple Choice - Podcast Script Features

Answer:
B. Clear structure and engaging language

Activity 5 : Sentence Sequencing - Storyboarding Process

Answer:
Correct sequence: 3 → 2 → 1 → 4

Activity 6 : Match the Pair - Elements of Interactive Fiction

Answer:
- A - 1
- B - 2
- C - 3
- D - 4

ACTIVITY CORNER 7

Activity 1 : Multiple Choice Questions

Answer:
1. b) Persuade the audience to take action
2. b) AIDA
3. b) Creates a direct, personal connection with the reader
4. c) Red
5. b) "Start your free trial today!"

ACTIVITY CORNER 7

ACTIVITY 2 : MATCH THE FOLLOWING

Answers:

1. d) "Sign up now and get 50% off!"
2. c) Evokes feelings to connect with the audience emotionally
3. b) Attention, Interest, Desire, Action
4. e) Writing that makes the reader feel directly addressed
5. a) "For sale: baby shoes, never worn."

ACTIVITY 3 : TRUE OR FALSE

Answer Key:

1. False
2. True
3. False
4. True
5. True

ACTIVITY CORNER 8

ACTIVITY 1: MULTIPLE-CHOICE QUESTIONS

Answers:
1. B
2. A

ACTIVITY 2 : TRUE/FALSE

Answers:
1. False
2. True
3. True
4. False

ACTIVITY 3 : MATCH-THE-FOLLOWING

- Image-Based: B
- Open-Ended: C
- "What If" Questions: A

ACTIVITY 4 : SEQUENCING

Answers:
1. **D**
2. **B**
3. **C**
4. **A**

ACTIVITY 4 : SEQUENCING

Answers:
- D
- B
- C
- A

ACTIVITY 5 : MATCHING SOCIAL MEDIA TYPES TO EXAMPLES

Answers:
- Caption: "An exciting moment captured: 'Life's better with friends!'"
- Blog Post: "10 Tips for High School Success."
- Tweet: "Finished my latest project – can't wait to share it with you!"

ACTIVITY 6 : IDENTIFY THE TYPE OF PROMPT

Answers:
1. "What If" prompt
2. Open-Ended prompt
3. Image-Based prompt

ACTIVITY CORNER 9

ACTIVITY 1 : MATCH THE PLATFORM WITH THE STRATEGY

Answers:
1 - B, 2 - A, 3 - C, 4 - D, 5 - E

ACTIVITY 2 : MATCH THE PROMPT WITH THE TAGLINE

Answers:
1 - B
2 - E
3 - C
4 - D
5 - A

ACTIVITY 3 : TRUE OR FALSE: BUILDING YOUR BRAND

Answers:
1. False (Instagram thrives on short captions or visually striking content.)
2. True (CTAs are essential for driving user action.)
3. True (Consistency builds trust and recognition.)
4. False (Storytelling helps simplify and humanize technical services.)
5. False (High schoolers can and have successfully marketed services online.)

ACTIVITY 4 : MULTIPLE-CHOICE QUESTIONS

Answers:
1. B
2. B
3. C
4. B

ACTIVITY CORNER 10

ACTIVITY 1 : WRITING A COMPELLING TWEET - MULTIPLE CHOICE QUESTIONS WITH ANSWERS

1. B
2. B
3. B
4. B
5. B

ACTIVITY 2 : MATCH THE FOLLOWING

Answers:
1. 1 - c
2. 2 - b
3. 3 - a
4. 4 - d
5. 5 - e

ACTIVITY 3 : FILL IN THE BLANKS

Answers:
1. Digital Storytelling
2. Blogging
3. YouTube Video Script
4. Gamified Content Creation
5. Educational Content Development
6.

CONCLUSION: CREATIVE WRITING FOR HIGH SCHOOL STUDENTS

As we reach the end of this book, we hope you now recognize the profound impact that creative writing can have on your personal, academic, and professional growth. Whether you're using it as an outlet for self-expression or a powerful tool for future career opportunities, creative writing is an invaluable skill that enriches both the mind and the imagination.

Throughout this book, we've explored various forms of writing, from traditional creative storytelling to modern techniques such as copywriting for digital platforms. By understanding writing fundamentals, practicing persuasive and analytical writing, and developing skills for the digital age, you've equipped yourself with the versatility needed for both personal expression and future professional success.

In today's world, creativity is a highly valued asset in every field, from marketing and entrepreneurship to content creation and digital storytelling. By embracing the techniques discussed here—from crafting engaging stories to mastering concise, persuasive language—you can shape your voice in the digital landscape and beyond.

We encourage you to continue experimenting with different writing styles, to take risks, and to always aim for growth. Use this book as a guide, and remember that creative writing is not just about producing perfect work, but about exploring ideas, experimenting with language, and pushing boundaries. The more you practice, the better you'll become at expressing yourself, connecting with others, and thinking critically. And who knows? The next great storyteller, copywriter, or content creator might just be you.

As you move forward, carry with you the understanding that writing is more than just a skill—it's a lifelong journey of learning, expressing, and evolving. Whether you're writing for a class assignment or creating digital content for the future, let your creativity soar and guide you toward endless possibilities. Happy writing!

We'd Love Your Feedback!

★ ★ ★ ★ ★

Please let us know how we're doing by leaving us a review.

APPENDIX -A :
CREATIVE WRITING FORMATS AND THEIR CHARACTERISTICS

Writing Format	Description	Examples	Key Features
Short Stories	Narrative writing that typically focuses on one event or character	"The Tell-Tale Heart" (Edgar Allan Poe)	Engaging plot, clear theme, limited characters
Poetry	Expression of feelings and ideas through rhythmic language	"The Road Not Taken" (Robert Frost)	Use of imagery, rhyme, and meter
Essays	A short piece of writing on a specific topic or idea	"A Modest Proposal" (Jonathan Swift)	Structured argument, formal tone
Scripts	Writing for performance, often dialog-heavy	"Romeo and Juliet" (William Shakespeare)	Dialogue, stage directions, character arcs

APPENDIX -B :
GRAMMAR AND PUNCTUATION TIPS FOR CREATIVE WRITING

Rule	Explanation	Example
Comma Usage	Commas separate elements in a sentence and improve clarity.	I love writing, reading, and painting.
Apostrophes for Possession	Use apostrophes to show ownership.	The student's notebook was lost.
Quotation Marks	Quotation marks enclose dialogue or direct speech.	"I can't wait to write my novel," she said.
Colons and Semicolons	Colons introduce lists; semicolons connect closely related sentences.	I have three loves: writing, reading, and traveling.
Active Voice	Active voice strengthens writing and makes it more direct.	"She wrote the novel." (vs. "The novel was written by her.")

APPENDIX -C :
WRITING TIPS FOR EFFECTIVE STORYTELLING

Tip	Description	Example
Develop Complex Characters	Characters should have depth and motivations that make them relatable.	Harry Potter's growth throughout the series
Show, Don't Tell	Instead of telling the reader how a character feels, show it through actions and dialogue.	Her hands trembled as she picked up the letter.
Use Conflict to Drive the Plot	Conflict creates tension and propels the story forward.	In "The Hunger Games," the survival conflict drives the plot.
Create a Strong Setting	The setting helps establish mood and can even act as a character.	The dark, stormy castle in "Frankenstein" adds to the atmosphere.
Focus on Structure	Break your story into beginning, middle, and end with clear transitions.	The "Hero's Journey" framework is a common structure in storytelling.

APPENDIX -D :
HELPFUL WRITING RESOURCES

Resource	Purpose	Website/Author/Publisher	Additional Notes
Grammarly	Grammar and spelling checker	www.grammarly.com	Helps with proofreading and grammar checking.
Hemingway Editor	Style and readability checker	www.hemingwayapp.com	Assists in improving readability and conciseness.
Writer's Digest	Writing advice and prompts	www.writersdigest.com	Offers creative writing resources and inspiration.
Thesaurus.com	Thesaurus for word choices	www.thesaurus.com	Find synonyms to expand vocabulary and style.
National Novel Writing Month (NaNoWriMo)	Writing challenge and community	www.nanowrimo.org	Aimed at helping writers complete novels in one month.

APPENDIX -E :
CAREER OPPORTUNITIES IN WRITING AND CONTENT CREATION

Career Path	Description	Skills Needed	Example Job Titles
Copywriting	Writing persuasive text for advertisements, websites, and marketing materials.	Creativity, persuasive writing, attention to detail	Copywriter, Advertising Specialist
Content Creation	Developing engaging content for digital platforms like blogs, YouTube, and social media.	Writing, video editing, social media skills	Blogger, Social Media Manager
Technical Writing	Writing user manuals, guides, and other documents that explain complex topics.	Technical understanding, clarity, organization	Technical Writer, Documentation Specialist
Scriptwriting	Writing scripts for TV, film, video games, or theater.	Dialogue writing, plot structuring, character development	Screenwriter, Playwright
Journalism	Reporting on news stories for print, online, or broadcast media.	Research skills, objectivity, communication	Journalist, News Writer

We'd Love Your Feedback!

Please let us know how we're doing by leaving us a review.

YOUNG WRITER SERIES - DR. FANATOMY

We'd Love Your Feedback!

Please let us know how we're doing by leaving us a review.

www.ingramcontent.com/pod-product-compliance
Lightning Source LLC
Chambersburg PA
CBHW082210070526
44585CB00020B/2356